Lyla Winn has teacher for over fifteen years and *I Dare to Share God's Gifts* is a collection of poetry that she has been sharing with her family and students for years. These poems have ministered and encouraged many different people as they pour out of Mrs. Lyla's passion and heart to serve the Lord in every aspect of her life.

Brad Smith
Minister of Children's Ministries
First Baptist Church Clarksville, Tennessee.

Lyla's poems are a ministry. God will put someone on her heart, and she will sit down, seek His face, and write what He gives her. Her poems have blessed, encouraged, comforted, and exhorted many people. Through the years, Lyla has often called me to be a sounding board, and as I hear her read her latest work, as only she can do, all I can say is, "That's beautiful, Lyla." It's always a blessing when I pick up the phone and hear Lyla say, "Do you have time to listen to a poem?"

Eloise Weatherspoon
Prayer Partner

I Dare to Share

God's Gifts

Lyla Winn

I Dare to Share

God's Gifts

Lyla Winn

Tate Publishing & *Enterprises*

I Dare to Share God's Gifts

This title is also available as a Tate Out Loud product. Visit www.tatepublishing.com for more information.

Published by Tate Publishing & Enterprises, LLC
127 E. Trade Center Terrace | Mustang, Oklahoma 73064 USA
1.888.361.9473 | www.tatepublishing.com

Tate Publishing is committed to excellence in the publishing industry. The company reflects the philosophy established by the founders, based on Psalms 68:11,
"The Lord gave the word and great was the company of those who published it."

Cover design by Lynly D. Taylor
Interior design by Janae J. Glass

Published in the United States of America

ISBN: 978-1-60247-814-5
1. Christian 2. Poetry
3. Inspiration

07.08.03

I dedicate this book to my Lord and Savior Jesus Christ.
It was all of Him and none of me.
He is the one to receive honor and glory.
He has always been my best Friend,
And I hope these words will inspire you
To allow Him to be yours too.

Recognitions

I would like to extend recognition to everyone who has ever been a part of my life, but that is impossible. So I will mention a few who have been so outstanding in my being able to accomplish writing this book.

First, I want to thank my husband, Charles, who has allowed me to spend so many hours on the couch reading God's Word, praying, meditating and listening for answers from God while he was busy doing my house chores and getting everything entered in the computer and printed.

Next, I would like to thank my daughter-in-law, Rae-ann, who compiled all the poems on the computer and helped me in so many ways to be able to do this book. She spent many hours when she could have been having fun with my beautiful grandchildren, Hayden and Emma, who are three and five years old, and her husband, my only son, Chad, my pride and joy.

Thanks to my niece, Jenny, who had to have a lot of patience with me while she was trying to edit and I kept changing things. She did it because she loves me and wanted me to stay alive through these words.

I want to thank all my children and their spouses for loving me and encouraging me. Especially my daughter, Teresa, who sang so beautifully in our church ministry and her husband, Gary, for allowing her to be a part of it and Jake and Josh, her handsome sons, for not complaining.

Thanks to my oldest daughter, Cindi, who is a nurse and tries to help keep me well, and her daughter, Cara, who also writes, and Cindi's husband, David, who loves them both very much.

Thanks to my daughter Dawn. She is my baby girl and helps with the housework for me and shares my beautiful granddaughter, Jaden, who's four. Also, to her husband, Billy, who does everything for everyone. He's one of a kind.

Thanks to Julie, Raeann's friend, who helped put it in book form so I could

get an idea of how it would look.

A very special thank you to Eloise, my dear friend, who took time while on her vacation to proof read my book.

To Jean, my sister, who has been a joy all my life. She pushed me to write this book and even helped with the financing. If it weren't for her, I probably would have given up.

I would also like to thank my prayer partners for believing in me and insisting I use the gifts God has given me and for all their prayers and suggestions.

Isaiah 55:11–12

So shall my word be that goeth forth out of my mouth:
It shall not return unto me void,
but it shall accomplish that which I please,
and it shall prosper in the thing whereto I sent it.
For ye shall go out with joy, and be led forth
with peace: the mountains and the hills shall
break forth before you into singing, and all the
trees of the field shall clap their hands.

Table of Contents

Foreword

"And we know that all things work together for good to them that love God, to them who are the called according to His purpose." Romans 8:28

> "So shall My word be that goeth forth out of My mouth: it shall not return unto Me void, but it shall accomplish that which I please, and it shall prosper in the thing whereto I sent it. For ye shall go out with joy, and be led forth with peace: the mountains and the hills shall break forth before you into singing, and all the trees of the field shall clap their hands." Isaiah 55:11–12

God alone can make "mountains break forth into singing

and the trees of the field to clap their hands." His Word is the greatest artistry and poetry ever written.

Lyla Winn is a child of God with the touch of His hand on her art and poetry. Lyla's heart is full of the love of God and overflows in her writings. Lyla has blessed me continually in these years serving as Pastor to her and her husband, Charles. This book of Lyla's poems will allow you to experience the love of God in a beautiful and fresh way.

God's greatest artistry will be seen when Romans 8:28 comes to full blossom in eternity. God will work all things together for good, even cancer and death. He will unfold an artistry so glorious that we will sing for eternity, "Oh, Lord my God…How great Thou art." Lyla, Charles, and all His children will sing the new songs of God in Glory one day soon! "Even so, come, Lord Jesus."

In Christ,

Dr. Roger P. Freeman, Pastor
First Baptist Clarksville, Tennessee

My Story

Where do I begin? Well, my name is Lyla Winn, and I have been born again. God forgave me my sins, and I began a new life way back then. He taught me that He was the only way and that I should always pray. He said He would never go away, but I must hear what He had to say, so I could obey. I started a new day. He has shown me when I am wrong, but He makes me feel like I belong. My Lord is so strong. I am sorry this took so long, but now I have a new song.

Now I am trying to let others know that He really loves them so. If they will just let go and stop feeling so low, that they too can start to grow, and Oh! what blessings He will bestow and what love He will show. I am so excited, you see, because He has been so good to me. I am not who I used to be. I have found Heaven's key. With this, you must agree.

So now I write about Him when things start to look dim, or if I am going out on a limb, and sometimes when I am being condemned, or just when I get a whim. I write inspirational poetry, you see. He has given this gift to me. It is a way for me to plea so that you will agree that the Lord can set you free, and make you what you ought to be.

So please don't start to flee. Because He gave His life for you and me when He died upon that tree.

You see, our Savior was crucified; He suffered and died so we would not be denied. But in the grave, He did not have to abide. He is now at God's side with His arms opened wide, waiting for you to let go of your selfish pride and let your soul be satisfied. Oh! please don't let these words slide. You will never have to be ashamed anymore, because you won't be the person you were before. You see, God has opened Heaven's door and He has so much in store. So please, don't put this off anymore. Your Savior, you will adore.

Poems from My Daughter Teresa & My Church Ministry

Thank You, God

Thank You, God, for inspiring me
And allowing me to write.
These words that I receive from You,
Make my heart feel so light.

I want to let others hear them,
Because I know in Your own way,
They too, can feel Your presence,
As they listen to what I say.

I know I couldn't write one word
If You weren't in control,
If these words were really mine
They wouldn't touch one single soul.

I know that You have all the answers
To every question in their hearts,
And only You can keep them away
From Satan's fiery darts.

So when they read these words, Lord,
Let them remember they came from You,
And give You all the glory
As they let Your love shine through.

Inferior

I've always felt a little inferior,
Because there are things that I can't do.
My abilities are a little limited,
And sometimes, I can't carry through.

Sometimes I get embarrassed,
Because I seem to mess things up,
And when I should be listening,
I always seem to interrupt.

But there is one thing I am sure of,
I have been born again.
So when I start to stumble,
God forgives me for my sin.

I'm thankful God gave me a gift
That I can carry through,
The ability to write a poem,
With the message: He loves you.

So I hope that you will enjoy them,
And let God's light come through,
So you can feel His presence
As I share them now with you.

Jesus' Love

Oh, don't you love to hear about Jesus,
And the way He loves you so?
Don't you really start to get excited,
When you learn things you did not know?

Sometimes I feel like laughing,
And sometimes they make me cry;
Especially when someone starts to tell
Of how my Savior had to die.

But it is really such a blessing
To know He died for you and me,
How He took our sins upon Him
As He hung upon that tree.

You know He did not have to do that.
Any angel could have taken His place.
But He knew He had to suffer,
So all our sins He could erase.

Oh brother, don't you love Him?
Don't you wish that you could be
Exactly like He wants you,
Because He alone can set you free.

God's Grace

Grace is a gift we do not have to earn
And a promise that never can fail.
It is a reward that all can experience.
It is an answer that all is well.

By faith, we can reach out and take it.
By patience, we can expect the best.
By prayer, we can release our burdens,
And our Savior will do the rest.

God's grace can free us from anger.
That is something our flesh cannot do.
We can relax in the arms of our Savior,
Because His grace will carry us through.

In my flesh, I can do nothing,
Because my pride gets in my way.
So isn't God's grace the answer?
Let us relax and accept it today.

Praise

Let us praise the Lord with all our hearts,
Because He truly deserves our praise.
He will always be here for us,
And in eternity, our bodies He will raise.

Let us praise Him when the world looks wonderful
And we feel we have no cares at all.
Let us praise Him when our world seems to crumble,
Because through praise, we will never fall.

Let us praise Him when He seems so far away,
And praise Him when we feel Him near.
Praise Him when we're full of grace,
And praise Him when we experience fear.

Let us praise Him when we're healthy and vibrant,
But also praise Him when we're racked with pain.
Let us praise Him when we can't see the rainbows,
And praise Him when the sun shines again.

Let us praise Him when man lets us down,
And praise Him for that special friend.
Let us praise Him when we feel so useless,
And praise Him for saving our soul from sin.

Let us praise Him for all the prayers He's answered.
Let us praise Him when the answers haven't come.
Let us praise Him just because we can trust Him;
Because without Him, nothing could be done.

The World Truly Needs King Jesus

JESUS, Oh, how I want the world to know You,
So that they will accept You as their Lord.
But how can I ever persuade them,
That You must be worshipped and adored?

JESUS, show me a way to help make them see
That You really will answer their prayers
And that You will make them feel whole again,
Because that is how much You really care.

JESUS, can't they see that time is what they need,
If they want to start their search for You?
Oh, how I wish they only knew
Just how much a little time could do.

JESUS, You gave us twenty-four hours a day,
So why can't they ever seem to find
A time to be alone with You to pray
And to get away from all mankind?

JESUS, they find time for everything else
That their flesh wants them to do.
Oh, Lord, why can't they realize
That Your Spirit must get through?

JESUS, they eat, drink, laugh, and play.
They sleep, work, and then go on their way.
Why can't they see their need for You?
Oh, Lord, Oh Lord, what can I do?

JESUS, how can I help them find Your love
If they won't even take time to look above,
So that You can let them know
That You really, really love them so?

JESUS, if they would only pray the sinner's prayer,
You will do the rest because You care.
You will give them peace they've never known,
And they will never again be alone.

A Little White Lie

"Be sure your sins will find you out,"
These words from the Bible we have read.
So aren't we a little worried, my friend,
About some of the things we have said?

We tell a white lie, it leads to another,
Before long we are in pretty deep.
We have hurt your name and brought someone shame
All because we are so weak.

Sometimes the truth is hard to tell
But a lie is the coward's way.
If we are guilty, we must admit it to God
And we had better do it today.

When we lie we are not in control
We are letting the devil have his way.
Can't we see he is the author of lies
And he makes us believe they are okay.

But soon no one will believe us,
And God says a good name is better than wealth.
So what in this world is worth living for,
If we can't even trust ourselves?

Adversity

How do you handle adversity, my friend?
Are you consumed with fears and doubt?
Or do you depend on the Lord for later reward
And trust until He gets you out?

God always wants our attention,
And sometimes we just won't obey.
So in order for us to listen to Him,
Sometimes He puts adversity in our way.

Troubles make us realize how much we need Him,
And that He is the only way.
So we must learn to live in those circumstances
By trusting Him more every day.

When we try to trust in our flesh,
This just does not work, my friend,
Because no matter how intelligent we are,
None of us can live above sin.

None of us can predict the future,
We don't even have a clue.
So why can't we just wait on God?
He is the only one who knows what to do!

Children Listen

Children, hear the Laws of the Lord
And stop lying to yourselves and others.
You only see life the way you want it;
You act as if your eyes are covered.

You don't want to hear what God has to say,
Because you don't want to change your ways.
You think you can put your trust in yourselves,
And just live your life in a daze.

If you just put your trust in yourselves
And don't try to see things God's way,
All you are doing is deceiving yourselves,
And the devil is having a heyday.

When you do hear a word now and then,
It seems to make you run farther away.
I think you are afraid you will realize what you are doing,
And that you might be tempted to obey.

You say, "Don't tell us what to do,
Just turn us loose to have fun.
We want to live our lives our way,
We are not ashamed of anything we have done."

Children, please listen to what I say,
Because I have heard from the Lord.
I sat at His feet and listened and learned,
And now I am reaping the rewards.

I must let others know what I have learned,
So I am writing the words God has given me.
I know you just think I am talking like a fool,
But I am going to keep trying to make you see.

Yes, you can act any way you choose
Because God has given you a free will,
But you also have to reap what you sow,
And that could be a pretty big field.

So, children, please take time to think,
Before you commit your sinful acts.
I am sure you will find God is on your side,
If you will just read the Bible for the facts.

God's Armor

When Satan shoots his fiery darts,
You don't have to be afraid at all,
Because you can put on God's armor,
And by faith, you'll never fall.

If you put the belt of truth on first,
You'll be reminded of what is true,
That God loves you with agape love,
And that He'll always be beside you.

You must put on the breastplate of righteousness,
So you'll be determined to do what's right;
And regardless of what it may cost you,
You'll never turn and run from the fight.

Then slip into those sandals of the gospel,
To prove you're available to be used.
Then ask the Holy Spirit to help you interpret,
So your words could never get anyone confused.

Then take up the shield of faith,
So you can trust God and God alone.
And by believing you can do all things through Him,
You'll never have to walk alone.

Then when you put on the helmet of salvation,
Thank God for setting you free.
And thank Him again for the Holy Spirit
That He sent to live inside you and me.

Then pick up the sword of the Spirit,
Which you know is the word of God.
And read about all His wonderful powers
That will help you escape the rod.

Then you'll be able to rejoice,
And your eyes will be opened to see
That the battle has already been won.
Christ died to set you free.

Jesus

Jesus. Oh, what a wonderful, wonderful name.
Oh, how I dearly love to repeat it.
I could just say it again and again.
No other name could mean the same.

My heart aches when I hear someone misuse it.
How could we possibly treat it that way?
His name should always make us feel humble,
Not just when we're using it to pray.

Sometimes God's name is even used in profanity;
This should never happen, my friend.
He always needs His name exalted;
We should never use it to curse men.

Taking God's name in vain, in any way,
Is a very serious act.
We will end up having to pay.
Don't take my word, go to the Bible for the fact.

Yes, this is one of the ten commandments,
Found in the book of Exodus with all the rest.
He said He will not hold you guiltless,
So let's not put God to the test.

He is the Lord and He is so worthy.
How could we possibly stoop so low
As to use His name so unwisely,
When He dearly loves us so.

So the next time we use God's name,
Make sure that we're not taking it light.
And also, if we hear someone misuse it,
Let's pray that they'll learn it just isn't right.

God's Book

How many Bibles do you own?
I believe most of you have at least two.
Why do you own those Bibles?
Are they really there to inspire you?

Or maybe you keep them on the shelf
Just in case the preacher comes by.
Could it be you think it is your Christian duty,
Or do you even know the reason why?

The Bible is the inspired Word of God
And the way for us to reach Him.
It holds answers to every problem,
If we will just look for them.

It tells us stories about the prophets,
And how they heard from God.
And it teaches us how we should listen,
So we can escape His chastening rod.

It also holds so many promises,
That our Lord will make come true
If we will just accept His love,
As He shows us what to do.

It tells us all about Jesus,
From His beginning to the end.
How He was born in Bethlehem in a manger,
And how He died for you, my friend.

So I challenge you to read God's book.
You will be so glad you did.
You will uncover so many wonderful things
That really should not stay hid.

Let Me Be a Light

God, help me to be and do and see and say
Everything I should today.
Let me smile and speak and reach out
To some lost soul who's feeling doubt.

Let me share the gifts that You've given me,
By reaching souls that need to be set free.
Let me give them hope and never despair
By letting them know You'll always be there.

Let me help them let go of their selfish pride,
So they too can feel Your spirit inside
And know that You are all they need.
Oh Lord, please help me plant a seed.

I just must be a light for You
Because You've shown me what to do.
By uncovering mysteries in Your Word,
I feel I now just must be heard.

So Lord, please guide me the way You choose.
Because if it's Your way, I cannot lose.
So direct my steps from this day on,
So I will know a seed I've sown.

Lift Up Your Pastor

Have you lifted your pastor up in prayer today
And asked the Lord to anoint him in a special way?
And to give him the exact words to say,
So you, his sheep, will never stray?

Have you asked the Lord to give him perfect peace,
So the devil's power just can't be released?
And that every thought of doubt or fear will cease,
So he can break the bread of life, so you may feast?

Have you asked the Lord to provide for his every need,
So he will be able to go where the spirit leads?
And have you asked the Lord to help him always heed,
And that he will be ever so willing to plant a seed?

Have you asked the Lord to have mercy on his soul
And to allow him to become brave and bold?
So he will have no fear of what the future holds,
And the old devil will never be able to take control?

Ask the Lord to help him stay healthy too,
Because he needs strength to minister to you.
Ask Him to give him grace to carry through,
And a clear mind to do all the things he must do.

Pray for God's wisdom that He sends from above,
Because it can only come through the power of love.
And ask him to use it to give you a shove,
Because God's wisdom is what this world is in need of.

Baptism

It is such an awesome privilege to be baptized
Because we are allowing the whole world to know
That we are willing to follow our Savior,
No matter where He wants us to go.

Did you know baptism is a Christian symbol
Done in obedience to our precious Lord?
We are baptized with water into repentance,
Getting ready to accept our eternal reward.

No, this water does not wash our sins away.
Only the Savior's blood could have done that.
But it is a way to let the world know,
That we are following the example He set.

Baptism is a symbol of being buried into death,
Never to be the same old flesh again.
But to be raised from death into His glory,
Having been forgiven for every single sin.

If you have accepted Christ as your Savior,
You should never put this off, my friend.
It is not only your privilege, but your duty,
And a message every Christian should send.

It allows the world to know you have been born again,
And that you never have to be afraid anymore.
This Christ-like act could change another's heart.
So Christian, tell me, "What are you waiting for?"

Come and Follow Me

Come and follow me, whispers Jesus.
Then you answer, I can't right now.
I'm too busy with the world, Lord.
Later, you can show me how.

Come and follow me, whispers Jesus.
And you answer, I can't just yet.
I'm too busy with my girlfriend,
But I promise, I won't forget.

Come and follow me, whispers Jesus.
Then again, you answer no.
I'm too busy with my job now.
Lord, I can't just let it go.

Come and follow me, whispers Jesus.
Then you answer no again.
I'm just starting a new family,
And I don't know where to begin.

Come and follow me, begs my Savior.
Come to me in your final days.
Lord, I'm too old to get religion;
I'm too set in all my ways.

Jesus smiles and says, I'm sorry,
Because I still love you so.
But I really need you to help me
Save your family from him below.

You see, you didn't take time to trust me,
And your family trusted you.
They thought you had all the answers,
Now it's too late to carry through.

Forgive

Is there anyone in our life that we haven't forgiven?
Is there something we are holding over someone's head?
Friend, if there is, we had better bring it to the surface
And deal with whatever words need to be said.

Did you know when we hold those hurts inside,
That we are the ones that really have to pay?
And if we don't deal with this problem
We might never have another joyous day.

With problems like these, we need assistance
From the Savior who had so much to forgive.
We must let him lead us to the solution
Because he is the only one who knows how we should live.

It is easy to blame someone who has hurt us,
But could it possibly be a misunderstanding on our part?
It really doesn't matter where the blame lies,
But we have to get it settled in our heart.

This is the day the Lord has made,
But how can we possibly rejoice in it
If we are carrying around those hurtful feelings
That we won't even let ourselves admit?

So please, let's not let pride get in our way;
Let's do whatever it takes to make things right.
God will show us exactly what to say
And brother, we will sleep better tonight.

God's Requirements

To act justly, love mercy, and walk humbly
Are acts that our precious Lord requires of us.
When I discovered this in the book of Micah,
I knew immediately these actions were a must.

Micah says He has shown thee, O Man, what is good,
And then explains what the Lord required of thee.
By this we will understand God's righteousness more freely,
If we will study and learn about all three.

We must look to the Spirit to interpret these words,
Because our own understanding is not good enough.
We must also wait and not get impatient,
And never give up when life gets rough.

To act justly means to treat others with fairness,
Without ever expecting anything in return,
And to listen instead of reaching our own conclusions.
Now that's a lesson most of us should learn.

To love mercy doesn't mean that we deserve it,
Or that we're just waiting to be showered upon.
It means we're willing to show mercy to our debtors,
And forgive them if they reap where we have sown.

To walk humbly before God is my favorite.
This I can learn as I spend time with God in prayer.
Humbly is the only way that I can approach Him,
Because He already knows why I am there.

But I need to be reminded how much He loves me,
And I need to express my love for Him.
I need strength that only He can give me,
So I'll be able to tell others how much He loves them.

Gifts from God

His wisdom, discernment, and judgment
Are precious gifts from God.
But reaching out to accept them
Makes the world think we're odd.

His Word has so many promises
That would make our lives complete;
But not having enough time and energy
Gives Satan another chance to defeat.

We will never know our strength
Until we let our weakness go.
We must become totally surrendered
Before we can really start to grow.

Why do we keep banging our heads
About the things that we don't know?
When will we finally learn,
Only He puts our ducks in a row?

When we try to get ahead of Him,
And start trying to impress others,
We haven't accomplished one thing,
Only confused our sisters and brothers.

So let's ask God to speak to us,
And not doubt that we will hear.
When we know He is our inspiration,
We'll stop accepting doubt and fear.

Daddy

Daddy, why do you drink?
My youngest child said to me.
It makes you act real mean,
And I know you don't want to be.

Daddy, don't you love us?
You are always gone from home.
Mama and us get scared sometimes,
When you leave us all alone.

Daddy, Mama's crying again.
You didn't hit her, did you, Dad?
Oh Daddy, what makes you drink?
It makes you act so mad.

Daddy, can we go to church?
Someone told me Jesus loves me.
I bet He loves you too, Dad,
Let's you and me go see.

They say Jesus watches over us,
And that He can make us free.
He might help you stop drinking, Dad.
Won't you please go with me?

They said they nailed Him on a tree,
And stood and watched Him die.
What's wrong, Daddy, is there something in your eye?
Oh Daddy, I didn't mean to make you cry.

Parable of Sower

Do you remember the parable of the *Sower*?
And how Jesus explained to the disciples so well,
That the seed sown was the Word of God,
And then He described where each seed fell?

Which one of these landing do you fall into?
Are you the Wayside, Rocks, Thorns, or Good Ground?
Please listen how He explains each one,
It might help you turn your life around.

If you're the *Wayside*, you've heard the Word,
But you didn't truly believe it from the start,
So you allowed Satan to come and take it from you,
Before you could apply it to your hardened heart.

If you are the *Rocks*, you received God's Word,
And even joyfully accepted it as true.
But you didn't take time to read the Bible,
So you fell away as soon as Satan tempted you.

Or could you be the *Thorn* who accepted it freely,
And really believed you had overcome your sin?
But you got caught up in the things of the world,
Instead of perfecting its fruit; eventually Satan won again.

If you're the *Good Ground*, you devoured the Word,
And believed without a doubt that it was true
You used it to become patient and willing,
And through the Word, God became a part of you.

Satan's Lies

What is wrong, little Christian friend?
Where is that sparkle in your eyes?
Don't tell me you are starting to doubt,
Or fall for Satan's lies.

Is he telling you that you are not really saved,
And that you are living a lie?
And does he remind you of all your sins,
And even make you cry?

Don't you ever let him lie to you,
You know Christ has set you free.
So the next time he starts to bother you,
Just tell him in Christ's name to flee.

Then turn your eyes toward heaven,
And thank Jesus once again
For helping you defeat Satan,
And for forgiving all your sins.

Widow

Oh widow, don't you weep no more,
Thy maker is thy husband now.
With great mercies He will gather you,
If you will but humbly bow.

When it seems no one doth care,
And you feel so all alone,
Your Heavenly Father is waiting there,
To be invited into your home.

No other one could love you so,
Or extend such constant care.
If you let Him gently guide you,
You'll always feel His presence there.

When life seems to be standing still,
And you feel you can't go on,
He'll be there through grief and tears,
Until He gently leads you home.

My Utmost for His Highest

If I could borrow the words of Chambers;
A pastor of great renown,
I too, would want to declare my utmost for His highest,
And allow Him to turn my life around.

I'd have to expect a change in circumstances,
But I'd never again have to be ashamed,
Because I would have found hope and understanding
And would realize there would be much to gain.

I would feel a boldness that I'd never experienced,
And I would know that I was magnifying my Lord.
I wouldn't turn and run when things got difficult,
I'd depend on His Word as my sword.

I would be determined to allow Him to use me,
Even if I didn't understand what was happening to me.
I would have learned not to lean on my own understanding,
So I would surrender my will and become free.

Yes, free to let go of everything around me,
So there would not be anything in His way.
Then the Holy Spirit would lead, guide, and direct me,
And I'd feel His presence all through the day.

I wouldn't worry anymore about what others think of me,
Because worry could take my mind off Him.
I'd just ask Him to let me remember
That He is always in control of them.

Through Him, I'd always make the right decisions.
I wouldn't be selfish anymore.
I would accept help from my fellow man
Instead of insisting on my way, as I have done before.

I'd learn how to be a good listener,
My ears would be open to God and man;
Instead of demanding that I be heard.
I would be more sensitive to God's plan.

I would never gossip about my neighbors
Because I'd really need them as my friends.
They might walk away and leave me,
And I would lose them in the end.

Yes, being able to accomplish His highest
Would be the best thing that could happen to me.
Because others would be able to see a difference,
And they too, could have this desire to become free.

The Lord's Wisdom

"This is the day the Lord has made,
Let us rejoice and be glad in it."
It is His day, not ours,
And He will use it as He sees fit.

We know His ways are not like ours,
Because the Bible makes that clear.
We must put ourselves into His hands,
So we will not worry, dread, nor fear.

Trust in the Lord with all your heart,
And lean not on your own understanding.
Put away your selfish pride,
And stop being so demanding.

"The Lord is my shepherd, I shall not want,"
Is a promise from His Holy Word.
So why can't we trust our Savior for our needs,
If He can feed a little bird?

Jesus says, "Blessed are the meek,
For they shall inherit the earth."
So why do we always try to take control?
What are our decisions really worth?

"Make a joyful noise unto the Lord,"
Now that is something we all can do.
And if we put our trust in Him,
He will make our dreams come true.

He says, "If we have the faith of a mustard seed,
We can move mountains."
And if we only believe,
We can drink from His fountain.

His wisdom is better than fine gold.
And His Word will prove it is true.
You can uncover mysteries for yourself.
Friend, the Bible is waiting for you.

Unlearning

Please release us from our own mindset, Lord,
And let us become more dependent on You,
Because things always seem to get harder,
When we allow our wrong thoughts through.

We have access to all God's powers
That we need to see us through,
But if we can't let go of our wrong thinking,
We miss getting our minds renewed.

We just can't live our lives our way
And expect things to turn out great.
We need God to use His powers,
As we sit and meditate.

The Holy Spirit lives right inside us
To guide us all life long.
But we must acknowledge His presence,
Before we can even decide right from wrong.

Do we really depend on our own mindset
Without questioning it at all?
Do we think that just because we thought it,
That it automatically became law?

We can never lean on our own understanding
So we have to learn how to obey.
Then we can break through our mindset,
And allow the Holy Spirit to have His way.

We must be willing to unlearn some deceptions
That we have let ourselves come to believe,
Things that only the devil could have planted,
Because he wants our minds deceived.

Unlearning is always harder than learning,
Because our mindset is so strong.
But we must ask the Holy Spirit to search us,
So He can tell us where we went wrong.

We might never be able to reach others,
Until we're willing to unlearn what we think we know.
Because some of those deep planted mindsets
Just won't allow God's seed to grow.

Willing and Obedient

If we will be willing and obedient,
We shall eat the good of the land.
God has given us this promise,
From the very beginning of man.

But do we know what this promise means?
Do we really and truly understand
That God must be first in our lives,
And that we must want to obey His commands?

We must accept Him as our personal Savior
And then allow Him to lead the way,
So that we can accept His promises,
And see miracles happen every day.

He will be everything we need in life,
And will make our lives complete.
But the only way that we can trust Him
Is to stay seated at His feet.

If we decide to use our own will,
He will let us walk away.
Because He doesn't make us do one thing,
We have to be willing to obey.

He only wants His name exalted,
And He will teach us what to do.
So there is no reason to be afraid
That we won't be able to carry through.

His grace is what He gives us,
That is how He makes our lives complete.
So won't you please just trust Him?
His love is "Oh, so sweet!"

Where Is Your Faith?

Where is your faith, my friend?
Do you put your faith in yourself?
Only to realize what a failure you are,
And end up feeling lost and empty.

Where is your faith, my friend?
Do you put your faith in man,
Trying to get a free ride to nowhere?
Because that is exactly where you are going.

Where is your faith, my friend?
Do you put your faith in your job
To give you a sense of worth,
Only to discover anyone can do it?

Where is your faith, my friend?
Is it all tied up in the things of the world
That fade away and leave you
And take your pride with them?

Where is your faith, my friend?
Is your faith in the Almighty God
Who loved you so much he died for you
So that you could live forever in peace?

Only through our faith in God
Can we discover "whose" we really are,
But first we must be able to let go,
And allow Him to completely take over.

Take a Stand

As we travel through this life
With so many worldly demands,
Let's remember whose world it really is,
And decide to take a stand.

We will never regret our choices
If we let the spirit lead.
And I promise we won't be disappointed.
He'll supply our every need.

We don't have to possess silver or gold
Or anything of that kind,
But to be a success in God's eyes,
We just have to draw a line.

So let's examine the life that we're living,
Are we all that we can be?
Or are we still chasing worldly dreams
That will never set us free.

You know we can make a difference
Throughout this almost hopeless land,
But if things are ever going to change,
We all must take a stand.

By trusting in our Savior's Grace
And not trying to walk alone,
We can make a difference
That will reach His heavenly throne.

So please sing this song with us
As we represent our precious Lord,
By trying to make a difference,
That people just can't ignore.

Let's all lift our voices bravely,
And let our message show,
That we're never going to compromise
Because we love Jesus so.

If things are even going to change,
We all must do our part.
So let's sing this song together
And mean it from our heart.

Don't Rob God

Do we give God a tenth of our earnings?
Can we trust Him enough to obey?
Or have we decided we just can't afford to,
Because we have too many bills to pay?

Did you know that if we refuse to tithe,
We're actually robbing our Lord?
It says so in the Holy Bible,
So these words just can't be ignored.

"Ye are cursed with a curse
For you have robbed me."
Yes, these words are written in Malachi,
For the whole world to see.

We must bring our tithes to the storehouse,
Which is the house of God,
Then we will be free to receive His blessings,
And escape His chastening rod.

The Lord asks us to let Him prove it,
So what do we have to lose?
We must give Him what belongs to Him.
There is really no other way to choose.

Then He will open the windows of Heaven,
And pour blessings down on me and you.
And we won't have room enough to receive it
If we will just do as the Lord says do.

So why would we want to keep His tenth,
When He has given us so very much?
If we really trust Him like we say,
His tenth we will not want to touch.

Who Deserves Heaven?

How can we ever deserve to go to heaven?
This is a question we all must ask.
We really have to know the answer
Because this day could be our last.

Do we think it is by keeping God's commandments
And living the very best that we can?
Or maybe we think it is by going to church,
Trying to serve our fellow man.

Do we think it might be helping the poor
Or by giving a tenth to our church?
Could it be we might need to teach,
Or are we still continuing our search?

Do we think we have to work real hard
In order to become worthy, my friend?
If we're really thinking this way,
We all must start over again.

There is only one way we can deserve Heaven
Because not one of us is worthy, you see.
And no matter how hard we try,
We could never be "as good as could be."

So God sent His only Son from Heaven,
Because He knew all our wicked hearts.
Our only hope was to accept Him as our Savior,
And allow Him to do our part.

So Jesus shed His precious blood
As He hung on that cross for me and you.
And that blood opened the doors of Heaven,
So you and I could go through.

Why Did He Have To Die?

I want you to go with me, if you will,
To an old rugged cross on Golgotha Hill.
Now picture our Lord, His body so still.
He died for you, friend; this scene is real.

They said He had lied, that He wasn't God's son.
They laughed and they scorned and made fun.
They didn't flinch as they watched His blood run.
They thought He had lost and they had won.

They never believed His words were true.
They didn't want Him telling them what to do.
They thought He was a man, just the same as you
And they didn't care what He was going through.

Now go with me to the tomb where His body lay,
And watch as the stone was rolled away.
God had no intentions of letting Him stay.
Jesus rose from that grave the third day.

Why did He have to die for you and me?
So He could forgive our sins and set us free.
Yes, now we can live victoriously,
By becoming who He wants us to be.

My Second Grade Sunday School Lessons

A Grateful Teacher

Dear Lord, I thank You for these children
That You allow me to teach.
Let me speak Your words of wisdom,
So their little souls I'll reach.

I know that I'm not worthy,
But You've given me this chore,
To get them excited about learning,
So that You can teach them more.

Lord, open up their little hearts,
And let Your light shine through.
Let me try to be a little spark,
That leads them home to You.

I know that I'm still learning,
And You know that I have to be led.
Oh! But if I could touch a single soul,
By something I have said.

I want to teach them how to love,
And that they must forgive,
So their lives can be an example,
Of how a child of God should live.

We Are God's Army

Children, can you hear me?
Are you listening when I say,
"Make every second of your life
A time to watch and pray"?

There's no time for bragging.
No time for telling lies.
No time for living Godless lives,
But a time to realize.

We have to work and watch and pray
And never stop to doubt.
We've got to keep pressing on,
While others walk about.

We're God's army, can't you see?
He needs us to work for Him,
There is a sinful battle going on,
And the future looks mighty dim.

That's why we can never stop to worry,
For there is victory around the bend.
We're God's chosen weapons,
And we must fight to the end.

How to Obey

How do I learn to obey,
When I can't hear God say,
"This is the way"?
Oh, I know! I will pray.

I can't hear God speak,
So His Word I must seek.
But my flesh is so weak,
How do I become meek?

I must have faith,
Before I can undertake;
Or I will make a mistake,
And His commandments I'll break.

One thing I can do,
I can learn what is true.
And by listening, I'll pursue.
Then my heart, I'll renew.

Will you help me to learn,
So that I can discern?
Then my heart will yearn,
To obey with concern.

Thank You

Two little words can mean so much.
You'll never know whose heart they'll touch.
Why do we find them so hard to say,
When they could change another's day?

A simple thank you means you were aware
Of that person that showed they care.
And that you acknowledge the things they do,
And the kindness they have shown you.

So always remember to say thank you,
For every small thing someone might do.
Because they will be encouraged by what you say,
And you'll be so glad you replied that way.

Thank you said, I noticed what you did,
You treated me with love and it wasn't hid.
You caused me to have a better day,
And a single thank you is all you had to say.

A Miracle

What is a miracle? one might ask.
Well, it's just God, fulfilling a heavenly task.
Now, was that so hard to understand?
God is a spiritual leader, not a man.

When you finally learn that He is in control,
He'll allow you to see miracles start to unfold.
Because faith in Him is all it takes;
So sit back and watch, for goodness sake.

Prayer can open your eyes, so you can see
Just how much He cares for you and me.
It releases His power and shows His love;
Then miracles start to shower from above.

And all you have to do is really believe;
And then by His grace, you will receive.
He even knows what you want before you ask,
So never doubt that He's equipped for the task.

Now doesn't this make you want to shout,
Now that you really know what miracles are about?
So just tell Him to send one your way,
And I'll promise that you'll receive it this very day.

Christ Is the Gift

What was the first Christmas gift,
And why was this gift sent?
If you know the answer,
You'll know what Christmas meant.

It has the gift inside its name.
Can you guess the answer yet?
It's also why we celebrate each year,
And the reason we must not fret.

This gift changed the whole world,
And set the prisoners free.
It also forgave us for our sins,
And made the blind to see.

It's simple. Christ is that gift.
Did you pass this test?
I hope you always thank Him,
As you open all the rest.

Have you accepted this gift,
And allowed Him to change your heart?
All you have to do is ask,
And He will do His part.

He'll send the Holy Spirit,
To tell you when you're wrong.
And He will always forgive you,
So please don't wait too long.

Palm Sunday

I was walking to Bethany,
When a colt I did see.
So I told the disciples,
To bring him to Me.

If the owner asks you why,
And I think he might,
Say, "Our Lord has need of him,"
And he will be alright.

So they untied the colt,
And brought him to Me.
On him, I would ride,
So everyone could see.

They spread some clothes
Over the colt's back
And also in front of him,
To look like a track.

When I got on the colt
And had started to ride,
A multitude of people
Were right by my side.

They were all waving palm leaves,
Then they began to rejoice,
They sang, "Praise be to God,"
In a real loud voice.

They called me a king,
And I thought that was nice.
Then they shouted, "Peace in heaven,
And glory in the highest."

The Pharisees were angry.
They said, "Make them stop."
I told them if I did,
They would hear it from the rocks.

Because I knew very well,
That they needed to see
That I was the Savior,
And that God had sent me.

Abram

Abram was a man of God,
And he lived in the city of Hayran.
God told Abram to go to a new land,
And he always obeyed God's command.

So he took his wife and nephew, Lot,
And his servants and all he had.
And started on his journey.
I'm sure that made God glad.

God told him He would be with him,
That He would never leave him alone,
And that he could teach others to worship Him,
And he would make His name well known.

When Abram came to Si'chem,
God said, "I'm giving this land to you.
It will be yours and your relations
To use any way that you want to."

So Abram built an altar there,
And worshiped and thanked God.
But he knew he wouldn't stay there,
They had farther on to trod.

They next arrived in Bethel,
So they built another altar and prayed.
Then they went from place to place,
Deciding where to stay.

But God led them back to Bethel,
Where they had built an altar there.
And that's where they would stay,
Because that was God's desire.

The Widow's Offering

One day, Jesus came to the temple.
He wanted to watch the people give.
So He sat across from the temple treasury,
Thinking about how these people live.

Some people were very rich,
And they had a lot of money to give.
They would have plenty left over,
So it wouldn't change the way they lived.

They probably gave to feel important,
Or to impress their fellow man.
It didn't matter what they had given,
Because they didn't really understand.

Then a little widow lady came by,
And she put only two coins in.
She didn't care who was watching her,
But Jesus' heart she did win.

She gave all the money she had,
Because she trusted in the Lord.
She wasn't worried about her lifestyle,
She had given all she could afford.

Jesus called His disciples to Him,
And He told them what she'd done.
Even though she just gave two pennies,
She had given more than anyone.

Centurion Soldier

Jesus was in the city of Capernaum.
Some men came to talk to him.
They knew a man that needed healing,
And wanted Jesus to go with them.

This sick man was only a servant,
But his master was an important man.
He was a Roman Centurion soldier,
Who was known throughout the land.

So Jesus started out with the men,
But they were stopped by a crowd.
They had a message from the Centurion
That made Jesus very proud.

The message read, "You need not come,
Your healing power has been revealed.
You can just speak a word there,
And I know my servant will be healed."

Jesus was amazed by the Centurion.
He knew that he really believed.
So when the messengers returned home,
The servant's sickness had been relieved.

Yes, Jesus healed the Centurion's servant,
Because he knew that Jesus could.
Don't you know that Jesus loves you,
So you must always try to do good.

Peter's Big Catch

"I'm going fishing," Peter said.
His friends decided they would go too.
So they all got into the boat,
And fished the whole night through.

They were very tired and hungry,
When they reached the shore the next day.
"Did you catch any fish?" a stranger asked.
They replied, "Not a one, we hate to say."

He said, "Put your net on the other side."
So they did as He told them to.
The net filled with so many fish,
They were afraid it would break through.

John realized the stranger was Jesus,
That had shown them what to do.
So Peter jumped into the water to swim,
So he could hurry to tell Jesus, "Thank you."

When the rest reached the shore,
They saw Jesus had built a fire.
"Bring some fish over here," He said,
"And we'll cook them if you desire."

Then Peter helped drag in the net.
153 fish filled it to the brim.
Then he took some fish to Jesus,
And He cooked them for them.

Jesus gave them bread and fish,
And they ate together once again.
They were so happy to be with Jesus,
And so glad to be called His friend.

Jesus Blesses Little Children

Jesus was answering questions
For people who were in doubt.
The questions were demanding,
As to what life was all about.

They sent their children also,
So He could bless them too.
But his disciples stopped them,
And wouldn't let them through.

This made Jesus very unhappy,
Because He loved the children so,
So He ordered the disciples,
To let those children go.

"Tell the children to come,"
He said with a nod.
"You must not forbid them,
For such is the kingdom of God."

Then He blessed the little children,
Oh how He loved them so.
Then the disciples were so sorry,
That they had forbidden them to go.

If Jesus loves you this much,
Don't you really want to do
Things that will make Him proud,
All the days that follow you?

Jesus Heals the Blind Man

I was walking down the road one day,
And I had a lot of followers with me.
Suddenly, I heard someone shouting real loud,
"Please help me, Lord, I cannot see!"

My people tried to quiet the voice,
But I knew it must be heard.
So I stopped to see who this was,
That needed me to speak a word.

He was sitting on the side of the road,
So I asked my followers to call him to me.
They told him to cheer up and get up,
Because I could make blind people see.

I asked him what he wanted me to do.
He replied, "Lord, I want to see."
I told him he could go now.
He would see because he trusted me.

He opened his eyes and looked around,
And sure enough, he could see.
He was so excited and happy,
He just couldn't stop following me.

Miracle of Loaves & Fish

A great crowd of people
Were following Jesus one day.
They wanted to see His miracles,
And hear what He had to say.

They had followed Him for hours,
So they were tired and hungry too.
He was pleased that they were listening,
And knew exactly what to do.

He asked Philip where to buy food,
But He knew he wouldn't have to.
He would perform a miracle,
And let them see what He could do.

Philip answered, "We have no money
To feed this hungry bunch."
Then Andrew said, "We have some food,
This boy has brought his lunch.

"He only has five loaves of barley,
And two small fish here.
Surely this can't feed them,
It's not enough, I fear."

But Jesus had the answer.
He said, "Make them sit down."
All five thousand people came,
And sat down on the ground.

Then Jesus broke the loaves and fish,
And after He had said a prayer,
Behold! There was plenty for everyone,
And even food to spare.

They gathered up the fragments,
So nothing would be lost.
Twelve baskets were left over,
All this without any cost.

So they knew Jesus was a prophet,
And they all believed that day.
They had seen a miracle happen,
That proved Jesus was the way.

Cornelius

Cornelius was a Roman soldier,
Who prayed to God every day.
He tried to keep his laws,
But couldn't see any way.

So one day, as Cornelius was praying,
An angel came to say,
"You must send for Peter in Joppa."
So Cornelius sent his messengers, right away.

Now Peter was on the housetop,
Waiting for dinner to be prepared,
When the Lord revealed to Peter
That the messengers were coming there.

God also informed Peter
That He loved all people the same,
And that he should go with the messengers,
So he didn't question why they came.

They took Peter to Cornelius' house,
And he told them that Jesus was Lord.
They believed him and were baptized,
Now they could all live in one accord.

The Prodigal Son

Jesus told a story
About a father and his two sons.
The youngest didn't want to stay home,
So he takes his inheritance and runs.

He went to a far away country,
And there he wasted all he had.
He lived a very sinful life
Because he hadn't listened to his dad.

Now he didn't know what to do,
He didn't even have a dime.
He knew he had to have food to eat,
So he took a job feeding swine.

Finally, he decided to go back home,
And bow at his father's feet.
He would ask to be his servant,
So he would have food to eat.

When he was in sight of his home,
His father ran to welcome him back.
He hugged and kissed him,
And the son didn't know how to act.

He told his father he was sorry
For all the bad things he had done.
So his father threw a party,
Because he had forgiven his son.

But the older son was angry
Because he had run away.
He was jealous of his brother,
Because his father reacted this way.

He said, "You never threw me a party,
And I was the son I ought to be."
But his father said, "But son, your brother
Was blind and now he can see."

Lazarus

Jesus had a friend named Lazarus,
That He loved very much.
Mary and Martha were his sisters,
And they always stayed in touch.

One day they sent a messenger to Jesus,
To tell Him Lazarus was ill.
The Disciples didn't want Jesus to go to him,
They were afraid He might be killed.

Jesus waited two days before leaving,
But He knew He had an appointment to keep.
He knew Lazarus had already died,
When He told the Disciples he was asleep.

When Jesus finally arrived in Bethany,
He knew that Lazarus was dead.
But Martha came to meet him,
And this is what she said.

"Lord, if only you had been here,
My brother would have lived,
But still, anything you ask of God,
I know that He will give."

When Jesus said to Martha,
"Thy brother shall rise again."
She asked, "On the resurrection day or now,
Lord, please tell me when."

"I am the resurrection and the life
And Lazarus shall live again.
Take me to the tomb,
And you will find out when."

When Jesus saw the tomb,
He could not help but cry.
He was very unhappy,
That Lazarus had to die.

"Take away the stone," he said.
"But Lord, his body is full of decay."
"I know," Jesus said to Martha.
"But you must believe God's way."

Then the stone was taken away,
And Jesus shouted into the air.
"Thank you for hearing me, God,
Now Lazarus, come out of there!"

"God, I know you always hear me,
But I want these people to see
That you're the one that sent me,
And that you can set Lazarus free."

Then Lazarus came out of the tomb,
He still was bound you know.
So Jesus told the people,
"Loose him and let him go."

So Lazarus was alive again,
And Martha and Mary were so glad.
And many people believed that day,
And turned from doing bad.

This is just one example
Of what our Lord can do.
If He can bring Lazarus from the dead,
You know He can take care of you.

The Ten Lepers

Ten lepers met Jesus in their village one day,
And asked Him to make their disease go away.
He told them to show themselves to the priest,
And they were all excited to say the least.

Because as they started out to obey,
Their skin became normal in every way.
One of them ran back and fell at Jesus' feet,
And the words "thank you," he did repeat.

Jesus said, "Stand up and go on your way,
You have truly been healed this day."
Then He asked, "Where are the other nine men?"
But the one couldn't answer for the others' sin.

Only one of the ten lepers had said thank you
When Jesus healed them and made them new.
What would make the others just walk away,
Without one word of gratitude that day?

Did the nine not realize that Jesus had healed them?
And that they truly needed to thank Him?
Or, was the lonely Samaritan the only one
That acknowledged Jesus as God's own son?

Go Teach

Disciples, you must hear Me,
Listen to every word I say.
Go into the world and teach
That Jesus is the only way.

Tell people I've gone to heaven,
But I haven't left them alone.
I'm sending the Holy Spirit,
To change their hearts of stone.

Tell them I'm always with them,
Because My Spirit will live inside.
Teach them all about Me,
And the reason that I died.

Teach them how to be baptized,
And to remember how John baptized Me.
This will prove they truly love Me,
And that I alone have set them free.

So Peter preached to thousands,
Telling them Jesus was the way.
And three thousand people believed,
And hung their heads to pray.

Then they all were baptized
Because they knew that was the way,
That they could show their obedience,
As they joined the church that day.

Peter Denied Jesus

Peter, how did you become so bold?
You denied my Savior I am told.
You couldn't have known what the future was to hold
When you allowed your heart to become so cold.

Your fears caused you to turn away
When your heart told you to stay.
You would never dream what part you'd play,
And that you'd give your life for Him one day.

Jesus, our Lord, wasn't at all surprised.
He had already told you that you would deny.
So when you saw the grief in His eye,
All you could do was run away and cry.

But thank God the story doesn't end there,
Even though you needed much prayer.
He knew you were in great despair
And just how much you could bear.

So after He had left His grave,
He wanted you to know that He forgave.
And that to sin you didn't have to be a slave.
The Holy Spirit would make you brave.

So Peter, He gave you a brand new start,
And you could boldly do your part.
You didn't have to prove you were smart,
Because now the Spirit was leading your heart.

Now He'd tell you what to say,
As you stood before the people at Passover that day.
Not once did you want to turn away,
You knew their thoughts you had to sway.

The Holy Spirit came into their midst,
Now your words they could not resist.
They knew that Jesus did exist,
And they listened at last and became His.

The Easter Story

God sent His only son to earth,
To sacrifice His life for us.
Even though He would be cursed,
He came so men could trust.

Some people gave their hearts to Him,
While others' hearts grew cold.
Some were afraid of His powers,
And what their future might hold.

So they nailed Him on a cross,
And laughed and made fun of Him.
They didn't realize they were lost,
And without Him, their future was dim.

The soldiers that nailed Him there shouted,
"Your God does not care!
If you were really His child,
He'd make you come down from there!"

But you see, Jesus had to die.
Because that was the only way,
That our sins could die with Him,
So we could be free today.

It was on a Good Friday,
That Jesus had to die,
They put Him in a new tomb,
As many watched and cried.

Sunday morning, the women came
And found the stone was rolled away.
They didn't know who to blame,
Or what had happened that day.

But suddenly two angels appeared and said,
"Tombs are for the dead,
Jesus is alive again."
Then they remembered what He had said.

"After I've risen again,
I will go before you into Galilee."
These were the words He had spoken,
So now they could clearly see.

He appeared again before many,
Before He ascended above.
They knew He had to go home,
But He had left below His love.

Cleopas and His Friend

Cleopas and his friend
Were walking down the road.
They were going to Emmaus.
They were talking as they strolled.

They said, "Jesus has been arrested,
And has died on a cross."
They had heard He was alive again,
So He could save the lost.

Soon a stranger came up to them,
And with them He started to walk.
They found Him very friendly
As He began to talk.

"Why are you sad?" He asked.
Cleopas answered, "Jesus is dead."
"We thought He was the Savior,
But His body is gone," he said.

The stranger told the men,
"Jesus was supposed to die."
Then He explained the scriptures,
And they knew He didn't lie.

Cleopas invited the stranger
To go home with him.
Jesus was happy to go,
So He could finish teaching them.

When they sat down to eat,
The stranger said a prayer.
After He had broken the bread,
Behold! He wasn't there.

They hurried back to Jerusalem,
And what a glorious reward.
To tell the disciples, "He has risen!
We have actually walked with the Lord."

Cleopas' News

Cleopas and his friend had seen Jesus.
When the disciples heard the news,
They were also very excited,
Because the truth they couldn't refuse.

Suddenly Jesus appeared before them,
"Peace be with you," He said.
They thought they were seeing a ghost,
Because some still believed he was dead.

"Do not be afraid," He said.
"I am alive, look at me."
Then they looked at His hands,
And nail prints they could see.

"Touch me if you want to,
You can tell that I am real.
I am also very hungry,
Could I please have a meal?"

They gave him some fish to eat,
And he ate like any man.
They said, "You are really alive.
You can eat just like we can."

"Don't you remember what I told you,
I am God's own son.
Don't you realize I forgive sins
And over death, I have won?"

"I want you to tell my story,
To the people of all nations.
So they too will believe in me,
Throughout all the generations."

Paul and Silas

Paul and Silas were preaching about Jesus.
Some people did not like the way they preached.
"Throw those men in prison," they shouted.
"We don't like the way they teach."

So, Paul and Silas were put in prison.
There they were beaten and chained.
They even had a jailer guarding them,
But they still prayed and sang.

At midnight, while they were praising God,
The prison shook from an earthquake.
Then the doors flew open,
And they could have escaped.

The chains also fell off them,
All the noise caused the jailer to wake.
He saw that the prison doors were open,
And he thought Paul and Silas had escaped.

He knew that he would be punished,
So he started to kill himself.
But Paul shouted, "Don't do that.
We're all here. No one has left."

The jailor was so grateful,
He said, "I know what I'll do.
I'll take you to my house,
And wash those wounds for you."

So Paul and Silas went home with him.
They must have talked about Jesus all night,
Because he and his family believed and were baptized.
Now they could worship God right.

In the Beginning

In the beginning, God created the heavens and the earth,
And the earth was total darkness, He confessed.
So He made day and night appear the first day,
And in only six days, He would complete the rest.

The next day, He made the air so we could breathe.
Then He made the earth from the dry land.
He made waters come together to make the seas,
And He did all this the second day, you understand.

The third day, He told the earth to grow plants,
So there were trees and plants all over the place.
He knew that His work was just getting started,
Because He knew He still had a lot of good space.

Now you must read the next week's lesson
To find out what He made the next day.
But if you don't get a chance to read it,
You can see the world turned out okay.

God Makes Man

God had made the sun, moon, and the stars.
He had made air, water, plants, and land.
He had made animals, fish, and birds.
And now He was ready to make man.

God needed someone to take care of the earth,
So from dust, God created man.
Then God breathed life into him,
But he needed a woman to finish His plan.

So God put Adam to sleep one day,
And took a rib from his side.
God made a woman from that rib,
So together man and woman would abide.

Then God put them in a beautiful garden,
And told them to take care of the land.
They also had to care for the animals,
This too was part of His plan.

There were also plenty of plant foods,
So they had plenty to eat.
God said, "What I have made is good,
And now I can rest my feet."

Jeremiah the Prophet

This story is about Jeremiah, the prophet.
A prophet is a messenger sent from God.
He repeats what God has told Him,
So that people can escape God's rod.

God told Jeremiah to write His message down.
So He told Baruch, his friend, to do the writing.
So Baruch wrote God's words on a scroll.
Now doesn't all this sound exciting?

Then Baruch took the scroll he had written,
And carried it to the temple.
He read it to all the people there.
Doesn't all this sound too simple?

The people knew the king would be angry,
So they told Jeremiah and Baruch to hide.
And when the scroll was read to the king,
Sure enough, he was fit to be tied.

Every time part of it was read to him,
He would cut if off and throw it into the fire.
Finally all the scroll was burned,
Because God's words he didn't desire.

But they couldn't find Jeremiah and Baruch,
So he couldn't punish them.
So Jeremiah and Baruch wrote another scroll,
And put more messages from God within.

Jethro Instructs Moses

Moses was the Hebrews' leader.
People would stand in line all day
To tell him all their problems
And to ask him to pray.

Jethro was Moses' father in law,
And he knew Moses needed help.
Although he was a great leader,
He couldn't do everything by himself.

Jethro told Moses to choose men
That would do their very best.
To help out with people's problems.
So Moses could get some rest.

Moses knew Jethro was right,
So he carefully chose good men,
That everyone could depend on.
Now he could relax again.

Now he spent more time with God.
And learned even better ways,
That they could fulfill God's will,
As they wandered out their days.

Moses

Moses had freed the Hebrew people;
He was ready to receive God's laws now.
God told him to get the people ready
And He would show him how.

Moses told them to get their hearts right
And he told them all God had said.
"Remember He brought us out of Egypt?
It was by His word, we were led."

Moses told them to wash their clothes
Because in three days they would meet him.
They were to stand in front of the mountain
And there God would speak to them.

So they did everything Moses had told them
And now it was time for God to appear.
They saw fire and lightning come down.
And they heard thunder in their ears.

Then they heard a trumpet sound,
And Moses was called up there.
So he went up on the mountain,
As the people stood and stared.

When Moses came down from the mountain,
The people were a little afraid of him.
But they listened to the ten commandments,
And promised to obey them.

Jonah Speaks

God wanted me to go to Nineveh,
Because the people there were bad.
He wanted me to tell them to stop.
I wouldn't go then, but I wished I had.

Because I decided to do things my way,
And not listen to Gods' voice,
I went the other way,
After all, it was my choice.

I got on a ship and went out to sea,
And a big storm started to blow.
The sailors were afraid they'd be killed,
So I knew I had to let them know.

I told them the storm was all my fault,
Because I hadn't obeyed my Lord,
And that the wind would stop,
If they threw me overboard.

So the sailors did as they were told,
And tossed me out to sea,
And sure enough, the sea was calm,
But guess what happened to me?

God sent a fish to swallow me
Because I had disobeyed His word.
I was in that fish three days and nights,
Until I decided God must be heard.

So he spit me out upon a beach
Because I was ready to obey.
I went to Nineveh and spoke for God,
This time I didn't run away.

The people listened to what I said.
They realized what they were doing was wrong.
They asked God to forgive them for their sins
And prayed and fasted all day long.

Naaman

Naaman was an army leader.
He was an important man you see.
But he was very frightened,
Because he had leprosy.

A young girl from Israel
Worked for Naaman's wife.
She lived in the house with them,
And feared for Naaman's life.

So she told her mistress
She knew a prophet in Israel,
And if Naaman would go to him,
She was sure he'd make him well.

So Naaman went to Israel,
Then he went to see the king.
But the king didn't know the prophet,
So he couldn't do a thing.

The prophet's name was Elisha.
He heard about Naaman,
So he sent a messenger to him,
Telling him what had to be done.

He said go to the Jordan River,
And wash yourself seven times.
Naaman was angry at first,
He thought Elisha was out of line.

But he went to the river
And did as he was told.
And the seventh time he came up,
His body was perfectly whole.

Gideon's Word

I went slowly toward the enemy camp.
I was sure glad the dark night hid me.
I stopped at the edge of the camp to listen.
A man was telling about a dream, you see.

As soon as I heard that man talking,
I knew what God wanted me to do.
So I went quickly back to my camp,
To tell my men what I knew.

God is giving us victory over the enemy,
So we must choose an army and go.
God has given me a sign,
And we will win I know.

So after I had chosen my army,
I put them in three groups you see.
I gave each man a trumpet, a clay jar and a torch,
And then I marched them off to the enemy.

When I gave them the signal,
They all started to blow.
And they broke those clay jars,
And the noise frightened the enemy so.

Then they held those fiery torches in the air,
And all shouted real loud.
They were so frightened then,
They just ran away from our crowd.

I was so happy I had obeyed God,
And used the talents He had given me.
I had helped my army win the battle,
Now my people could be free.

Nehemiah

Nehemiah worked for the King,
And he was quite content there,
Until he heard from his home in Jerusalem.
Things had happened that he wasn't aware.

The city wall had been torn down,
So his people weren't safe anymore.
The king asked him why he was sad.
He told the king God had given him a chore.

"I have to rebuild the wall of Jerusalem,
If you will release me to go.
I've prayed that God would be with me."
And the king just couldn't say no.

Some people there tried to stop Nehemiah
From the task God had given him to do.
But half of Nehemiah's workers stood guard,
So the enemies couldn't get through.

It took fifty-two days to rebuild the wall,
But Nehemiah knew it would get done.
He knew God was on his side,
So he wasn't afraid of anyone.

If you will always follow God's lead,
He'll help you with what you need done.
Ask Him to help you complete your work,
And there will always be time left to have fun.

The Ten Commandments

God gave Moses the ten commandments,
On that mountain long ago,
Because He knew that we must follow them,
If we ever intend to grow.

He knew we must learn to live
By rules that weren't set by man.
So with His Holy Finger,
He wrote down His commands.

He knew that we'd be tempted
To worship others in His way.
So the first and second commandments warn
That there is only one God to obey.

In His third and forth commandments
He asks us to reverence His name.
And to keep His Sabbath day Holy,
By worshiping and praising as our aim.

The fifth one of His rules
Is that our parents we obey.
It was the first command with promise
That a long life would come our way.

Thou shalt not kill is the sixth law.
It says we have no right to take
A life that God had created,
This would be a big mistake.

Do not commit adultery
Is seventh on His list.
Be true to the one you marry
So God's words don't try to twist.

The eighth is do not steal,
Don't take what is not yours to take.
You'll end up with nothing,
If you make this mistake.

The ninth command tells us not to lie.
He makes this very clear.
He says we can't get into Heaven,
If we don't get forgiveness here.

The last commandment tells us not to lust,
Or want what others have acquired.
If we trust God to supply our needs,
We'll have everything that we desire.

My Personal Psalms

A Child of the King

Sometimes I feel like I am a failure
Because of my limited abilities.
But then, I realize I have learned a great lesson.
It is not what I am, it is "whose I am."

I did not have to be a lawyer
To learn the Ten Commandments.
I did not need to be a doctor
To know that God can heal.

I did not need to be an actress
To learn the lines of scripture.
Nor did I have to be a professor
To profess the loving Savior.

I did not have to be an engineer
To discover God's perfect plan.
I did not have to be a scientist
To uncover all His blessings.

I did not need to be an astronaut
To enjoy His heavenly bodies.
So I have decided to be happy,
Just being whose I am: a child of the King.

Time with My Savior

When I wake up every morning,
The first thing I want to do
Is spend time with my Savior,
While my coffee starts to brew.

Nothing else seems to matter,
As I start out that way.
I forget about my troubles,
As I sit there and pray.

I get this wonderful calm feeling,
As the Spirit seems to say,
"Tell Jesus all your worries,
And He'll wipe them all away."

You know how much He loves you,
He's proved it many times.
He even writes your poetry,
And makes sure that it rhymes.

Oh, I know I'm not perfect,
And I'm sure that He does too.
But love can cover all my sins,
And make me feel brand new.

Self

Sometimes life seems like an incurable disease,
Because of situations that happen each day.
Things seem to get harder to understand,
When we try to live our lives God's way.

No matter how hard I try to obey,
Something happens and I end up defeated.
Someone seems to misunderstand my intentions,
Because of something stupid I've repeated.

I also seem to get frustrated so often,
And that, too, makes me worry.
Oh, how I wish I could feel at ease,
But it seems I always have to hurry.

I wish I would just depend on God's grace,
So I wouldn't make all these mistakes.
Why can't I just relax in His arms
And let His love overtake?

I really want to be an example for others,
So they can see Jesus working through me.
But I always let self get in the way,
And Lyla is all they are able to see.

But Lord, I'm not giving up.
One day Your words will come true.
I'll give up trying to depend on myself,
And let Your grace come bursting through.

A Lesson

I have learned a lesson,
So I must make others see.
Not one soul is perfect,
But God can set you free.

I carried around so much guilt,
Even as a little child.
I wanted so badly to be good,
And to make my life worthwhile.

When I accepted Jesus as my Savior,
I felt His love inside.
And I knew I would go to heaven,
Where Jesus does abide.

Oh, how I wanted to please Him,
Because He loved me so.
But no matter how hard I tried,
I couldn't let those guilty feelings go.

I just couldn't feel worthy,
No matter how hard I tried.
I felt I had let someone down,
Or that I had too much pride.

But my Savior was wonderful,
And He never left my side,
No matter how guilty I felt
Or how many tears I cried.

He showed me many wonders,
Even miracles I did see.
But I felt I didn't deserve them,
Because I wasn't as good as I should be.

Every day I studied and prayed
That God would teach me to be
More and more like Jesus,
So I could finally be free.

I really tried to be obedient,
And to do His perfect will.
I even taught Sunday School,
But I didn't feel worthy still.

One day I opened the Bible,
And to Isaiah I did turn.
God opened these guilty eyes,
And a lesson I did learn.

It's God's righteousness, not ours
That makes us what we should be,
So I can't hold on to condemnation.
God sent His son to set me free.

A Special Night

I looked in a mirror, and what did I see?
Without a doubt, it was an image of me.
I didn't like that face that was staring at me,
But why couldn't I accept it and just let it be?

My reflection in a mirror was only surface, I knew.
So what did God want me to do?
My physical appearance, I couldn't change at all,
But inside my heart, I heard God's call.

My heart was so heavy I began to cry,
And suddenly I noticed the tears in my eyes.
Why was I crying, I asked out loud;
And why did I suddenly feel humble, instead of proud?

When God opened those red swollen eyes,
I felt as if I had just won first prize.
I will never forget that very special night,
When God assured me that my soul was alright.

Battle Ground

My life seems like a battle ground,
With no one on my side.
Everyone seems to ignore my words,
No matter how hard I tried.

I search and search for answers
That will somehow make things clear,
But no matter what I seem to do,
I keep clinging to my fear.

I can't break this bondage,
That has become my way of life,
Because my faith isn't strong enough
To fight this weakness and strife.

My family thinks that I am wrong
By clinging to God's Word.
They think that I am a hypocrite,
But I know that God has to be heard.

I didn't have the patience,
That I should have had for them.
When they didn't understand God's ways,
I know I had to stand up for Him.

I knew He had all the answers,
That they so desperately needed.
But when I tried to explain faith,
My efforts were always defeated.

My life didn't represent the peace,
That He can so freely give.
Because I couldn't seem to grasp
The way He wanted me to live.

I couldn't seem to accept the gifts
That I know He had promised me.
And that I knew if I could only believe,
My life would be rich and free.

I wanted to prove that He's all they need,
So they'd stop clinging to earthly things.
And if they would accept His ways,
There would be no end to what He brings.

I never discovered the answer
So I gave them to the Lord.
Only he could ever persuade them
That he must be worshipped and adored.

Climbing Mountains

Good morning, sweet Jesus.
It's time to start our new day.
You take the lead, Lord,
While I stop to pray.

You know the way, Lord,
Much better than I,
So if You take the lead
We'll head for the sky.

Let's climb mountains together
Until we reach the top.
Oh, we really must get started,
There is no time to stop.

Oh it's beautiful up here, Lord,
So peaceful and quiet.
But I can see down below,
And it looks almost like night.

They're going in circles, Lord.
They can't find their way.
So we must go back, Lord,
They need us today.

But we'll climb more mountains
And maybe next time
We'll bring others with us,
When they've learned how to climb.

Dreams

There are so many things that I want to do,
But there is no way I can accomplish them all.
I am just not capable of following through,
My flesh is so weak, I always fall.

God has shown me it is not by my power,
And He's shown me it's not by my might.
He has shown me it's only by His grace,
So why do I still put up a fight?

Why can't I just trust His Spirit
And stop trying to depend on myself?
I only end up not accomplishing my dreams,
I just keep putting them on the shelf.

Oh Lord, I've been waiting so long
For my dreams to become reality.
I keep praying for the time and energy
That will never come to me.

I must go in the strength of Your Spirit,
Or my dreams will only stay dreams.
No matter how bad I want them to happen,
They'll never become reality it seems.

But now that God has shown me
That His Spirit and I make a team.
By accepting God's grace and not waiting on strength,
My dreams will not be worldly schemes.

Fear

I hear the voice of fear.
It's deafening my ear.
It's all that I can hear.
Nothing else can be heard.

No, not a single word.
Lord, this is so absurd.
I need to hear Your voice,
But with fear I have no choice.

It won't let me rejoice
I want to praise Your name,
But as long as fear remains,
My words become mundane.

How do I quiet this pain,
So I can start to hear again?
This fear is driving me insane.
How can I just let it go?

Why does it seem to grow?
Lord, I know You know.
The answer is in Your Book.
Oh Lord, please help me look,

To search out every nook.
Your Word will set me free,
You've promised this to me.
Thank You for hearing my plea.

Finally Free

Is this really too good to be true?
Am I really finally free?
Is my flesh nailed to Calvary,
So that I can worship thee?

I feel like I have just been born,
Because of the excitement I feel.
I am living for the first time,
Lord, this is really real.

I'm more relaxed than I've ever been,
Because I know you lead the way.
Now I realize You are the potter,
And I am only the clay.

This freedom I feel is so exciting,
There are no pressures from above.
All I have to do is accept life,
And I can experience Christ's love.

I want others to find this haven
That I have finally found.
I want them to know that Jesus
Can turn their unfruitful lives around.

Forgive Me When I Judge

God, thank You for loving me,
Even though I make mistakes.
I can ask for forgiveness,
And You'll forgive me for Christ's sake.

My flesh is so very weak,
But my Savior was so strong
When He died on that cross for me,
To forgive me of all wrong.

So forgive me when I judge my children,
I'm not worthy to judge anyone.
I'm just trying to direct them to You, Lord,
So they can realize what they've done.

Then they can turn their eyes on Jesus,
So that they may clearly see
That this world holds many dangers,
And He alone will hold victory.

God, I just want Your name exalted,
I'm not trying to put them down.
I just want them to see their failures,
And exchange them for Your crown.

Then they won't have to feel guilty.
They won't have to carry shame.
They can be gloriously forgiven,
If they ask You, in Jesus' name.

Then they can find the answers
That the world has never heard,
Because they will search the scriptures,
And learn to take You at Your word.

Freedom Praise

I will praise the Lord by singing
The words that He has given me.
Let us exalt these words together,
So we can lift our voices and feel free.

Let us know that this freedom we have
Comes directly from God.
And we must show others the reason,
That we have escaped His rod.

No other source in this world
Can keep up from all the destruction.
Oh, how we need to praise His name,
For allowing us to see His perfection.

He will shelter us under His wings,
He tells us in His holy book.
So we must trust His wonderful grace,
No matter how bad things may look.

He's a wonderful, gracious, loving savior,
And we need to witness for Him.
If we don't represent Him as holy,
How can our future not look dim?

I know that I know that I know,
So I must make others see,
That no matter how bad things may be,
Our Savior can set them free.

God's Help

As I travel down this earthly path,
Lord, I know You will help carry my load.
For only then will I have strength enough
To help the lost carry theirs.

Lord, I thank You for Your provisions.
You always take care of my every need.
Now I can have time to help those
Who haven't accepted Your help yet.

Thank You for taking care of me financially,
So my mind will be clear and alert.
And I will be able to understand why.
When others have lost everything.

Let me be a light to bring them back,
When they can't see Your provisions,
And can't understand the way,
That leads them to their heavenly possessions.

Gratitude

Lord, please give me an attitude of gratitude,
As I start out each day for You.
Let me be willing to accept my life
By allowing Your Spirit to see me through.

Let me always remember to be grateful,
Even though it's not meant for me to see
The reasons for each trial of the day,
To make me grow to be more like thee.

Lord, You have given me so very much,
I look all around me and feel so blessed.
I must accept every buttercup You offer,
And be willing to surrender to each test.

You are a God of mercy, grace, and love,
And You have promised I can receive them all,
If I will just keep on being persistent
And keep getting up every time I fall.

Why shouldn't I have to experience suffering,
And who am I that I should complain?
I'm growing in faith as I experience each burden,
And I'm thankful for all the wisdom I've gained.

I want to be more like Jesus,
I know this is the only way to get there.
Now I can share Your message with others
When they haven't suffered enough to know You care.

Heaven

I get to go to Heaven,
And walk Your streets of gold
You have given me this promise,
That this my future holds.

I get to see You, Jesus,
Even look upon Your face.
I get to put my crowns
At Your feet, as I am embraced.

I get to feel worthy,
Finally know that I'm okay.
I don't have to fear,
That You will turn away.

I will get to see myself
The way You look at me.
And I will finally love myself,
And, yes, I'll feel free.

I'll get to just be myself
And know that I have won.
I won't have to feel lazy,
Because of You, God's son.

You went before me,
When I couldn't find my way.
And You sent me mercy,
When I let You down each day.

I know that You love me,
You've proven it in every way.
I watched miracles happen,
And You made everything okay.

He'll Set You Free

I accept Your help, Lord. You're in control.
I can feel Your presence down in my soul.
Lord, this has always been my goal,
I knew someday You'd make me bold.

I can let go and feel Your peace,
And all my worries will start to cease.
With my flesh, they only increase,
But with my prayers, You're sweet release.

Why should I worry, fret and complain
Instead of calling on Your dear name?
I've been guilty, Lord, I repent in shame,
My soul was innocent, my flesh was to blame.

So I nail my flesh to the cross again,
Because there, it can't cause me to sin.
And I can expect to always win,
Because You, God, are my very best friend.

And only You can make life worthwhile,
You will turn my tears into smiles.
You will stay with me through every trial,
And once again I can live in style.

I love You, Lord, I trust Your ways,
And want to live out my final days,
Releasing my tensions and giving You praise,
And defeating Satan and his fiery blaze.

With Your peace my dreams come true,
Because then, I really depend on You.
Satan's rays can't get through
If I allow You to tell me what to do.

When I feel I can't go on anymore,
I always hear You knock at my door.
And I remember how it was before,
And so I trust You even more.

"Let go of your troubles," You whisper to me.
"You're my child. I'll set you free.
You're the child I want you to be,
So don't worry, I'll never flee."

His Love

I must spread good news about Him,
Because He let me feel His love.
I must share this special blessing,
That has come directly from above.

He's allowed me to discern the reason
That I can truly trust His love.
Because when I know I can't do anything,
It's then, He gives me a little shove.

He doesn't really need me anyway,
I will just get in His way.
He alone can make things happen,
If I'll allow His love to stay.

I must forget about past failures,
And I must put away my fear,
And just accept each one of His promises,
And realize that He's really near.

His love for me is overwhelming,
There's no way I'll let go of it.
Not one earthly thing can matter,
When at His beloved feet I sit.

Holy Spirit

Holy Spirit, You're such a blessing.
You are too wonderful for words.
How can I ever explain You to others,
If Your voice they've never heard?

How can I describe these feelings
When I really don't understand myself?
I just know I would never trade them
For any amount of this world's wealth.

When I have allowed anxiety to take over,
Because my flesh is so very weak,
Suddenly I realize I'm out of control,
So Your heart I begin to seek.

Now there's no way to explain my feelings,
It's all too wonderful for me.
You give me peace, love, and assurance
That You can set my anxiety free.

I realize when I let You control me,
I'm not afraid of life anymore.
And if I keep my eyes off myself,
Then Your Spirit can let me soar.

Only then can I experience Your miracles
Because by faith, I've opened a door
That my flesh could never have opened,
And I can walk where I couldn't before.

Jesus, thank You for the Holy Spirit.
You knew we couldn't walk alone.
Our flesh is so weak, we'd never be able
To find our way to Your heavenly throne.

So Lord, I ask You to let me be willing
To be led by the hand of God.
And let my flesh be nailed to the cross,
So I can escape the chastening rod.

I Will Not Cry

I love You, Jesus,
I will not cry.
I will lift my eyes,
When I start to sigh.

I will stop that tear,
Before I let it fall.
Not because I am brave,
But because You are my all.

When I feel so weak,
Lord, let me pray
That Your strength will come,
And make me strong today.

Let me praise Your name,
For all Your care for me.
Let me stop to think,
That I have been set free.

Show me the joy You left,
When You died for me.
You died so I could live,
And live victoriously.

Don't allow my weakness,
To take away that joy
Let me stop and thank You, Lord,
For all things you employ.

I know that I am blessed,
And You love me so.
That is why I cannot cry
Or let my weakness show.

I Won't Give Up

I won't give up, I must go on,
These words have become a part of me,
I know there is a reason for this waiting,
But Lord, what can it be?

I feel I am ready to share Your words,
So that souls might be set free.
But I can't seem to let go and let You
Decide what is best for me.

I feel like nothing is happening,
And I feel depressed in my soul.
I can't explain this anticipating,
But it's really taking its toll.

I feel that I am so useless
Because all I ever think about
Is when is it ever going to happen,
God, why do I carry this doubt?

When are You going to use me?
Do I really deserve the chance?
Why am I consumed with these thoughts?
Am I just a victim of circumstance?

You promised You'd go before me,
And that You would mark the way.
So why do I feel these heavy burdens,
That something must happen today?

I know I'm in the hand of the Potter,
So why do I try to mold?
I know I must wait for Your timing,
To discover what my future holds.

Lord, please reassure me again,
That things are going as planned.
And soon I'll experience rainbows
If I don't let go of Your hand.

Increase My Faith

Lord, please increase my faith,
I'm afraid it is too small.
I'm ready to climb mountains,
But I'm still afraid I'll fall.

I know without a greater faith,
I might try to depend on myself.
And eventually I would fall,
And You'd have to put me on the shelf.

Lord, I really want to be used,
But I feel so tired and weak.
I guess I sometimes feel hopeless,
And forget I have to seek.

Seek first the kingdom of God
Must echo through my heart.
It's You who can renew my strength,
And give me a brand new start.

Jesus' Lamb

Jesus loves me just the way I am,
Because He knows I'm like a little lamb.
Always getting myself in a jam,
Never confident, just feeling overwhelmed.

Being ashamed because of my pride,
Makes me want to go somewhere and hide,
Instead of running to His sweet side,
Where I know I would become satisfied.

He's just waiting for me to let go,
And realize I will never start to grow,
Until I learn to live in life's flow,
And stop holding on to what I know.

He's the answer to all my dread,
If I'll stop trying to push ahead,
And just accept that I'll always be fed,
If I'll remember to always be led.

He's the way, the truth, and the light.
When I learn this, I'll sleep well at night.
Knowing that I don't have to do everything right,
Because my sweet Savior has won the fight.

Just Fly

Push me out of the nest, Lord.
Please push me out of the nest.
It's time that I spread my wings,
And put them to the test.

I feel so very comfortable here,
And You've fed me with the best,
But it's time to spread my wings now,
Lord, I know You'll do the rest.

While I've been so helpless,
You've never once complained.
You've just covered me with Your wings, Lord,
And sheltered me from the rain.

You've taught me that You love me, Lord,
And taught me how to love.
Now it's time to leave the nest
So go ahead, give me wings like a dove.

Things look so scary down below,
I'm not yet sure I understand
Where my fight will lead me.
How can I know just where to land?

I really feel weak, Lord,
I'm just too afraid to fly.
But it's so beautiful out there,
I must be willing to try.

Will You fly underneath me, Lord,
So I won't be afraid?
You know all about this world,
That You so wonderfully made.

I must trust You completely,
And never start to doubt.
So push me right now, Lord,
I know it's time to go out.

I know my flight might not be easy,
And there is a chance that I might fall.
But if You're right there beside me,
You'll hear me when I call.

Lord, I knew You would never push me.
I had to do this on my own.
I decided to use my free will.
So thank God, I've finally flown.

Just Forgive

I want to live my life for You, God,
Because You are so good to me.
When others let me down,
I can always run to thee.

Lord, I am going to trust You,
So I really must let go
Of these terrible feelings,
So I can start to grow.

I have so many things to learn,
And time is running out.
I just don't have time and energy
To sit around and pout.

So Lord, please help my husband,
And show him he is wrong
And let me just forgive him.
So that he'll know who's really strong.

Leaning on God

Lord, I can't lean on my own understanding,
So I must lean on You.
Because I don't have the foggiest idea,
Of how I will be able to get through.

But Your Holy Word is filled with promise,
I know I've not even read them all.
And even though I can't imagine why,
You've promised You won't let me fall.

I can't depend on myself or man,
Because we're all just made of clay.
But You're the one that made us, Lord,
You can make everything turn out okay.

If You can make a lame man walk,
Or make the blind man see,
Or make this beautiful world in six days,
Then You can surely help me.

My eyes have been blinded
And I guess I've tried to walk alone.
You will forgive me for my ignorance,
If I'll let You rule my home.

Then I won't try to understand my life
Or judge the ways of man.
If I'll only stop and worship You,
You'll share with me Your miracle plan.

Let My Light Shine

Lord, let me be a little light,
To someone who has lost their way.
Let Your Spirit make the pathway,
When they can't tell night from day.

When they think there is no answer,
And all their hope is gone,
Let me be there to remind them,
That You will make them strong.

Let me help them on their journey,
Because I've been there many times.
Let me help them find the stairway,
That I have found to climb.

So that when they are weak and weary,
And can no longer depend on man,
They can cling to their only victor,
And that is Jesus, God's chosen plan.

Light Heart

If I could sit at Your feet all day
Nothing could go wrong.
No one could cause me to turn away,
Because I'd be where I belong.

But I must share this day with others,
Who haven't been with You.
Who haven't felt Your tender love,
Or asked You what they should do.

They've never felt Your loving touch,
Nor cried those tears of joy.
Or felt those heavy burdens,
For some little girl or boy.

So, I can't sit here, my dear Savior.
I must go and try to do my part.
If I follow Your directions,
I might help to mend a broken heart.

I might even get the privilege
Of sharing Your precious love,
So that someone else will have the feeling
That You're watching from above.

I thank You for the strength You give me.
And I pray I'll use it right.
Let no one be disappointed in me,
So that my heart can stay this light.

Loved Ones

Lord, show me a way to reach a loved one.
Let me, by Your hand, be led.
I know without You I can do nothing.
So please guide me so they too can be fed.

I just can't keep this to myself, Lord,
All this wisdom I have learned.
When my friends and family need You,
Lord, help me to be more concerned.

Do I lift them up before You
Each and every day?
Do I speak a word of kindness,
Or do I sometimes turn them away?

Lord, I know You are the answer,
But how can I make them see
That You can make a miracle,
And that You can set them free?

My Cup

I am feeling a little heartache,
And it's trying to get me down.
But I know if I trust in Jesus,
He's going to turn my life around.

I know things look a little dim now,
And I can't seem to find the way.
But my Savior's eyes aren't blinded,
And He hears me when I pray.

I must keep my eyes upon Him,
No matter how bad things may seem.
Because He's opening doors right now,
To help accomplish my every dream.

I'm sorry I'm so impatient, Lord.
I should just put my trust in You.
Because You know how this will end,
And You'll be there to see it through.

Lord, just allow me to feel Your love,
And accept Your cup with cheer.
And know that in Your right time,
You will take away my fear.

My Home

Lord, I want my home to be a haven,
To all who come inside.
I want every room to be opened,
With nothing there to hide.

I want to fill it with laughter
And music from the heart.
I want love to shine forth
And Your will to impart.

I want to welcome strangers,
Never turning anyone away.
But let them always feel welcome,
If they decide to stay.

I want them to feel Your presence,
That's my greatest wish of all.
Because if You don't live here,
This house would just be walls.

My Wish

I wish that I could be,
Exactly like You want me.
I wish that I could do,
Everything that would please You.
I wish that I could say,

The exact words You want me to pray.
I wish that I could know,
How You want me to grow.
I wish that I could go,

To the places You already know.
I wish that I could sow,
Words that seem to flow.
I wish that I could hear,

A word from You so clear.
That there would be no way,
That I could disobey.
I wish I'd stop depending on me,
So You would set me free.

Now I Pray

Jesus came into my life,
He came to set me free.
And no matter how I feel,
He's always there for me.

If I need a helping hand,
I turn my eyes on Him.
And He always has a way out
Without breaking off a limb.

When my body seems to balk on me,
I just look up and say,
"Jesus, what's Your answer?"
And He whispers, "Now you pray."

My body is still tired
And things are still not done.
But when I feel His presence,
Then I know that I have won.

My body may not feel good,
But my soul is satisfied,
Then I stop and whisper,
"Now I know why You died."

Oh Jesus, I Need You

Jesus, please help me when I am too tired
To do all the work that I know is required.
Sometimes I feel like I'm coming unwired.
Oh Jesus, Oh Jesus, I need You.

I look all around me, and what do I see?
All of these people, depending on me.
I don't have the time, Lord, to answer their plea.
Oh Jesus, Oh Jesus, I need You.

Where do I get the strength that I need
To finish my work, or to do a good deed?
I know You're the answer, but how do I heed?
Oh Jesus, Oh Jesus, I need You.

There are so many things that I can't seem to do.
I feel like a failure for not carrying through.
I want to do better, because I love You.
Oh Jesus, Oh Jesus, I need You.

When I get to heaven, I know I will hear,
"I love you, my child, and I hold you dear."
But I'm sure I'll whisper in my Savior's ear,
"Oh Jesus, Oh Jesus, I need You."

Questions

Do I believe every word of the Bible is true?
Do I question God's point of view?
Do I realize I'm a sinner through and through,
Or do I think I'm right in everything I do?

Do I know Christ died on a cross for my sin?
And that's the only reason I'm clean within.
Did I really confess and start a new life then?
And realize Satan could never win.

Did I accept His blood to cleanse my soul,
And allow the Holy Spirit to take control?
And did I start then to allow Him to mold
So I'd be an example of blessings untold?

Is my life dedicated to doing what's right,
Or do I still want to put up a fight?
Do I ever stay awake at night,
Asking God to improve my spiritual sight?

Do I know that I must be fed
By God's words, not earthly bread?
Or do I always seem to dread,
Reading the Bible or hearing it read?

Do I give back to God what He's given me?
Because He has allowed me to really see,
That giving Him His tenth is really the key,
To becoming the person He meant me to be.

Do I go to Him for everything I need,
And allow Him to always lead?
Or do I depend on myself and try to succeed,
And end up defeated because I didn't heed?

Am I honest with myself and others as well,
Or am I not even aware of the lies I tell?
Don't I realize how so many have failed,
And ended up in a burning hell?

Do I really care what kind of life I lead,
Or do I use others just so I can succeed?
Never considering what they might need.
Always trusting in self, not trying to heed.

If any of these things are true,
Friend, there is still plenty of hope for you.
Repent right now and ask God what to do,
Because self and man don't have a clue.

Please allow Him to change your heart,
By letting Him do His part.
Friend, He can give you a brand new start,
And only by God's wisdom, can you ever be smart.

Salvation

My mouth is confessing.
My heart is believing.
So this is salvation,
I now am receiving.

I yearned for the day,
That I would accept You;
But now that it's happened,
What must I do?

I know I'm not worthy
To be called Your child.
So maybe I won't tell,
At least for a while.

But I'm too excited
To keep this inside.
Oh! Help me, Jesus,
With my selfish pride.

You know all about me,
And you still hold me dear.
My sins are forgiven,
I don't have to fear.

I feel so grateful
That You set me free.
I didn't deserve it,
But You did it for me.

I have to show others,
That You love them too.
And they can be saved,
By believing in You.

Then their mouth will confess,
And their heart will believe.
That it's really salvation,
That they have received.

Song in My Soul

There's a song in my soul,
That needs to come through.
I must not hide it any longer,
Because the world needs to hear it too.

I can't keep it to myself any longer,
I must turn it loose to be free.
I know that it can help others,
Just the way it has helped me.

I feel someone is hurting inside,
And my song can ease their pain.
I'm sure it can bring some sunshine,
To help dry up all the rain.

Will you please share my blessings
As you listen to the words,
That God has given me to share?
They really, really must be heard.

They really are so simple
But you must apply them to your heart.
And by trusting in your Savior,
Decide to do your part.

These words have to be acted upon,
Or they will only be words.
And they have to be shared with others.
Yes, they really must be heard.

The song in my soul is this:
Jesus died to take away your sin.
And He wants you to love him
And stop feeling so condemned.

Struggling

Take these tears from my heart, Lord,
They're causing it to slide.
And before long, I'm afraid I'll falter,
And start flowing with the tide.

I'm so tired of trying to hold on.
Lord, it seems it's been so long,
That I've had to struggle this way.
Why are things going so wrong?

All I have ever wanted,
Was to know that you approved of me.
But the older I seem to get,
It's harder to believe I'll become free.

If I could have just one wish,
I wouldn't hesitate at all.
I'd ask to have peace of mind,
So that I could carry out my call.

I want to trust my mind to you,
I've misused it for so long.
I always think instead of act,
And cause Your plans to be prolonged.

I allow Satan to condemn me,
When I know I've been set free.
I don't have to live in condemnation,
If I'll open my eyes and start to see.

Lord, You are all I'll ever need,
So I really have no need to dread.
Why can't I trust Your word,
And know I'm being fed?

You love me just the way I am,
No matter what Satan tries to say,
I'm going to listen for Your voice only,
And these blues will melt away.

I still don't know why I struggle,
When I should live by faith alone,
But I'm asking You to forgive me,
When I try to live life on my own.

Things would become so easy,
If I'd just remember who You are.
My God and my Savior,
My bright and shining star.

Sunshine in the Storm

You are my sunshine in a storm.
You are my rainbow after the rain.
You are my rest after hard labor.
You are the healer of my pain.

You are my brother in time of need.
You are the friend I want to be.
You are the words I must heed.
You are my salvation, rich and free.

You are the way, the truth and the light,
That guides me through the day.
You are my light switch at night,
That clearly shows me the way.

You are the provider of my needs,
When I see no possible way.
You will always take the lead,
If I will but follow and obey.

You are everything to me, Lord,
And I want the world to know.
Without You I would be nothing.
Oh Lord, I love You so.

Surrender

Father God, direct my steps,
And let me forever be true.
There are so many ways I fail,
So I must trust in You.

I just can't reach the goal I set.
I seem to let everyone down.
I love You more than anything,
But I don't deserve to wear Your crown.

You are always there to assure me
That Your love for me is true.
But I act as if I'm all alone,
Instead of putting my trust in You.

Why do I let this lack of strength
Come between everything I desire?
Why can't I overcome like You did,
And do the things that are required?

I'm sure You didn't want to suffer
As You hung on that cross for me.
But You knew God wouldn't let You down,
And You knew He'd set You free.

I know God really loves me,
And that makes me feel even worse.
When I seem to sit and do nothing,
Always putting myself first.

God, only You know the answer
How will all this guilt end?
Will I ever be what I should be?
Will I ever understand why I sin?

Will I ever stop being lazy,
And let You use me in some way
That will make a difference,
In this world I live in today?

Forgive me, my precious Savior,
I know I must hurt You so.
Because You know I do love You,
But I just can't let go.

I don't even know what's holding me,
But Lord, I know I don't feel free.
Because my strength fails me,
I am not what I should be.

Lord, let me please surrender
And let me be able to see
That I can make a difference,
Because You can do it through me.

Your Direction

The next time I sit at Your feet
And start to praise Your name.
I'll be there for Your direction,
So I won't have myself to blame.

Lord, You know I want to do Your will,
And I want others to hear Your call.
Help me to do things that'll make a difference,
So I can help someone before they start to fall.

You've shown me Your wonderful miracles,
And You've shown me mysteries as well.
I have felt like I've almost touched heaven,
So Your story I know I must tell.

So open the ears of my listeners,
And give them a chance to see
The reason that I'm so excited,
About living my life for Thee.

Let me remember as I sit at Your feet,
And start to praise Your name.
That I'm there to get Your direction,
And that's the reason that I came.

Encouraging Words

I want to be an Encourager

Lord, help me to be an encourager
To anyone who is feeling down.
Let me try to show them Your love
And help turn their thoughts around.

Let me help them to see a brighter side
To anything they might be going through,
By looking to You to find peace of mind
And to help them stop feeling so blue.

If I can help them get their thinking straight,
Maybe they will begin to see Your light.
And realize that You are their best friend,
So they will stop feeling so much fright.

Lord, You know I still need encouraging too.
Sometimes I can't take my own advice.
I also need someone to lift me up
After I've fallen once or twice.

But thank God, I belong to You.
That's why I want everyone to know,
That You are there in good times and bad,
As we all continue to grow.

A Heavenly Message

You are a pastor with a gigantic heart,
Who has a deep love for God and man.
I know you're trying hard to direct your sheep,
But there are a few things you must understand.

I have a plan for each one of those sheep,
And I have to reveal those plans to him.
They must be responsible for hearing from Me,
So please stop trying to do that for them.

Some of My plans you couldn't possibly understand,
Because not one of those sheep are the same.
Only faith in Me will allow them to fulfill
Their dreams and their vision and My aim.

Some of them worship Me a little differently than you,
And you must stop letting this cause you pain.
Just feel privileged that you've led them to My throne.
After all, isn't that the reason that they came?

You must accept each of those sheep as they are,
And just open up your heart to every soul.
No one will ever interpret My Word the same,
So stop trying to make them fit your mold.

They all respect you or they wouldn't be there.
So, please, pay them the same respect.
Don't burden them down about the way they worship,
By putting your personal yoke around their neck.

You are a Spirit-filled man, led by My hand;
But not even you have all the answers to life.
None of your ways are like My ways,
So don't allow your conclusions to cause strife.

They gather in the church to worship Me.
Don't you know that's the reason they came?
If they're listening to My voice and allowing Me to lead,
Then your message in life has been proclaimed.

A Special Friendship

You're strong and enduring,
And giving and nice.
You're helping and willing
To offer much needed advice.

I appreciate your friendship.
You are one of a kind.
A more dependable person
Would be so hard to find.

That's why it's so important,
That you're soon feeling great.
We all need your guidance,
So we can hardly wait.

You have the courage that it will take
To endure the set-back with hope.
And you will keep pressing on,
You will never sit around and mope.

So today I'll say a special prayer,
That God will make you whole.
And you just have to keep the faith,
And allow Him to touch your soul.

Accept His Plan

Do you want to live your life in fear,
Or do you want to see a rainbow ahead?
You really do have a choice, my friend,
But you must listen to what Jesus said.

He said He will go before you,
So let Him always take the lead.
And don't doubt that He is in control,
Or that He'll supply your every need.

Tell Him that you accept His love,
And tell Him how much you love Him.
Then when you truly believe
Your fears will become very dim.

Acts of Faith

This little gift is to let you know
That through faith this seed I sow.
When things aren't perfect below,
Acts of faith teach us to grow.

It allows us to be a part
Of bringing joy to another's heart.
And stops Satan from routing the chart,
By trusting God to make a new start.

God knows that your heart is sincere,
So He will take away that fear
And dry up all those tears,
Because His provisions are already here.

In His timing He will release
All those blessings and perfect peace.
And all that anxiety will start to cease
And, oh, how your faith will increase.

Allow Him

Remember back to a time in your life,
When you were lost and bearing your own pain.
Then Christ set you free by His blood,
And now only shadows remain.

Praise God, your sins are forgiven.
He graciously paid all your debt.
And now you have discovered a wonderful freedom,
And there's no more room for regret.

You've found hope in His precious love.
You're depending on Him to make you whole.
You know He has taken over your life,
And you'll belong to Him, body and soul.

Yes, now that you've chosen His way,
You're on the road to a wonderful peace.
You are discovering things in your life
That you must allow Him to release.

You may have old chains that must be broken.
And you may have fear that you must let go.
But faith is stronger than bondage,
So turn loose and start to grow.

America

America, we have a new song to sing,
We must not accept the old one anymore.
If we will resist the devil's interpretations,
We'll sing words we have never sung before.

He's been choosing our words far too long.
We must refuse to listen to him roar.
If we'll sing as God inspires us,
Soon our words will start to soar.

We must sing with great authority,
Which we received from Christ our Lord.
And we must never become afraid
That our song will be ignored.

If we will open up our mouths to sing,
We'll learn new words as we go.
We must believe these words are life,
That we are learning as we grow.

Will you sing this new song with me?
Together, we will touch Heaven's gate.
Angels may even help us sing
The words that God will appreciate.

New song, new lyrics, and new meanings,
Experiences that your faith is living,
New mysteries that your mind has grasped,
And a way to express a new way of giving.

Our words don't have to be the same.
In America, we all have a voice;
But when we come together in harmony,
The results become God's choice.

This new song will lead us to freedom,
And also bring peace and good will.
If only we will do away with the old,
That came to rob, kill, and steal.

Thy kingdom come, Thy will be done,
Must echo through our song.
Out with the old, in with the new,
And we'll never choose the wrong.

Come on, let's sing our new song now,
And be determined in our hearts.
Thus, our song that we are singing,
Will give America a brand new start.

Brother Robertson

Brother Robertson, you don't even know me,
But God has put a burden on my heart
To keep praying for you continually,
Until you put the horse before the cart.

You can't keep trying to hold on
To the people who are dead.
You need to preach to the living,
In the way that you've been led.

You must not become weary,
Those people need you so.
Some may choose to leave,
But feel free to let them go.

So don't get discouraged,
You've been speaking from your heart.
The Holy Spirit is leading you,
And He has been from the start.

Thank Him for His precious Word,
And keep on daring to impart
All those words of wisdom,
Even when you don't feel so smart.

This world is truly in need,
And their eyes are too blinded to see.
You must keep trying to reach them,
So they can become free.

The Holy Spirit has to do the work,
But how can they ever learn,
If a pastor doesn't try to teach them,
With words he's been able to discern?

So, I hope you feel encouraged,
By these words I've been led to impart.
Don't let Satan get you down,
I know you have God's heart.

Cara

Cara, see how much you are loved?
Now you can come to understand,
That you have always been admired,
And that everyone thinks you're grand.

We want you to see yourself as we see you,
And accept the fact that you're the best.
So just hang in there and fight,
Because God has allowed you to take this test.

It may be the hardest one you've ever taken,
But just think what you've already learned.
You haven't had to face one day alone,
And through God, the answers you will discern.

By keeping a positive and determined attitude,
You will become a role model for all your friends.
You'll be the one that will always be appreciated,
Because you'll be the one wearing the biggest grin.

Now you'll do things you didn't have time for before,
Like reading a great book or writing a new song.
And if you stay busy and keep your mind alert,
You'll be healthy and strong before long.

You are beautiful inside and out,
So don't you ever start to doubt.
Accept all the beauty God has given you,
And you will have learned what life is all about.

Claire

Claire, My dear sweet little child,
You are so very precious in My sight.
I love you with all My heart,
That's why I watch over you day and night.

Claire, I know you cannot see Me,
But I am the one who helps you breathe.
And I am the one who keeps you fighting,
So you won't give up and not believe.

Claire, your mommy and daddy are My friends,
We've known each other for a long time.
That's why I have entrusted you to them.
But remember all of you are still Mine.

Claire, you don't ever have to be afraid,
If you will choose to think good thoughts,
And be willing to work real hard,
Because you have so much to be taught.

Claire, I've sent someone to teach you to talk,
And someone who will help you learn to stand.
So one day you'll be able to walk,
Without anyone holding onto your hand.

Claire, I'm asking you to depend on Me,
When you're tired or just feeling bad.
And to remember I'm always with you.
Even when you feel a little angry or sad.

Claire, You Can Pray

Claire, God can hear you talk to Him.
He knows everything you think and say.
Remember how you used to sit with Mommy,
And repeat the words you used to pray?

You are as sweet and beautiful as ever.
You are still the Claire you've always been.
So when you start to feel a little sad,
Tell Him to make you feel happy again.

Jesus loves you as much as we do,
And He will always stay by your side.
Don't you worry about walking now,
Soon you will be going for a ride.

Claire, we want you to think happy thoughts.
Just imagine angels watching over you;
And while you're waiting to feel better,
You can just sing the whole day through.

Close Your Eyes

Go to sleep, my darling,
Just close those pretty eyes.
Jesus is watching over you,
This you must realize.

He will give you lots of grace,
Because He loves you so.
Close your eyes and tell Him,
That you are willing to let go.

Allow Him to lead you home,
Where all His saints have gone.
You will hear the angels singing
And, oh, what a beautiful song!

Jesus will meet you in the sky
With His arms open wide.
And you won't have one single pain,
Because He'll keep you by His side.

So go on to sleep, my darling,
Don't worry about me.
Soon, I will come to join you,
So we can be together eternally.

Dr. Brannen

Dr. Brannen, I want you to know you are the best.
As a dentist, you are far above the rest.
As a Christian, you passed God's test.
Your fruits show all His righteousness.

Every time I enter your office door,
I feel God's presence and it makes my spirit soar.
I've never experienced this in an office before,
But that isn't all, I have to tell you more.

You have Bibles and Christian literature everywhere.
We can learn about God while we're waiting there.
This shows me how much you really care,
Because this office scene is very rare.

You're just as professional as you can be,
Yet you still find time to be kind to me.
I'm so thankful you received that dental degree,
With this, I know, all your patients agree.

God has given me a gift to write,
And I'm so glad you were my subject tonight.
Because today you made my heart feel so light,
And your gentle ways took away my fright.

Ella and Johnny

We have two really good friends,
Ella and Johnny are their names.
They're always visiting people,
And everyone is proud they came.

They're always thinking of others,
And what they can do for them.
They love to talk about Jesus,
So others will learn about Him.

They're always there when needed,
And I know they really care.
They're not there out of necessity,
And people like that are rare.

Ella crochets little Bible markers,
They're always in the shape of a cross.
She gives them to everyone she knows,
And doesn't even consider the cost.

She took a poem I had written,
And needle pointed and framed it for me.
It took three days to do it,
And I was as excited as I could be.

Johnny and Ella have the gift of help,
So they could use it for Him.
Jesus didn't give me that gift,
But I can write a poem praising them.

Eleanor and Frank

I would like to introduce you
To my sister and brother-in-law.
I have always admired both of them.
Perfection is what I always saw.

My sister has a place for everything
And everything had better stay in place.
If things aren't going well,
You can see it in her face.

But the world that she lives in
Is the place I long to be.
She always enjoys the outdoors
And the thought of being free.

She doesn't seem to be getting older
And she also lets you know
That you must never slow down,
You have to keep on the go.

My brother-in-law means the world to me.
He's so exciting to be around.
He's always doing something nice,
And his energy also does abound.

Sometimes my husband gets a little mad,
Because I think he's the perfect man.
But I'm sure he must be jealous,
Because he just doesn't understand.

Frank was good to me when I was little,
When I needed someone to lean on,
Because Daddy was always feeling bad,
And I knew to leave him alone.

So Frank made us feel happy
By showing us how to have fun
And I know that is the reason
That our hearts he always won.

Well, I love them both so much
And I love every one of you
So let's all be happy together,
And thank God, He's brought us through.

Friend's Night

Please look all around you, now what do you see?
So many unfamiliar faces, and that really shouldn't be.
Everyone of us here should be determined to find
A new friendship tonight, and one that will bind.

But we must be determined that we'll do our part.
Even if we have no earthly idea where to start.
If we'll just allow the Holy Spirit to show us the way,
That friendship will start, maybe even today.

We're here because each one of us has found
That God was able to turn our whole life around.
So now we must work together, so each one can say,
I want to share Jesus' love with someone new today.

He gives us words of wisdom, that others need to hear,
And He sends us friends to help soothe away our fears.
So we must reach out a hand of fellowship today,
Because tomorrow God could call any one of us away.

So tonight, walk up to someone you don't know,
And just release God's love and let it start to flow.
Then allow His wisdom to really shine through,
Because that's the only way they can meet the real you.

Generosity

My mind cannot fathom your reasoning,
For extending such a service as you do.
You work so very hard to serve others,
And all you receive is a thank you.

You are each so talented and wonderful,
To give of your strength and time.
Your generosity is so overwhelming,
And you never ask for one dime.

You make me feel such gratitude,
From experiencing this blessing from you;
And I am sure that so many others
Feel exactly the same way I do.

How can I express my appreciation
To people who are so generous and kind?
I am so glad that our hearts are united
By a tie that will always bind.

God's grace, and mercy, and goodness,
I want to extend to every one of you;
And I pray that you will recognize
What wonderful things you do.

Get Well Soon

I'm so sorry you're not feeling well.
Is there anything I can do?
Can I offer you a helping hand?
Or just write a poem for you?

Thank God I can pray for you,
Because He hears our every call.
I'm sure you will be better soon,
Because He really loves us all.

So while you're feeling poorly,
Accept some of His strength today.
He knows everything you are in need of,
So why don't you stop and pray?

God loves you all so dearly
And He wants the best for you.
So prayer is what I have to offer,
Because God knows just what to do.

Getting Older

How do you feel about getting older?
Do you worry and fret and complain?
Or do you just think you're getting closer
To completing this life and its strain?

Yes, we strain every day to do better,
And we mope if we make a mistake.
We treat life like it's a bad dream,
And we're just anxiously waiting to awake.

We worry that someone will notice
That we can't even remember their name.
And we feel that we're really worthless,
As we nurture our aches and pains.

Everything seems so much harder to do,
And suddenly our energy is gone.
We feel that life is passing us by
And wonder if we'll even live very long.

We feel like life is such a burden,
As we drag through another day.
We feel like we haven't accomplished a thing,
Oh! There must be a better way.

We know there is victory in Jesus,
But it must be after we die,
Because we can't seem to even handle today,
And sometimes we don't want to try.

We need to find that victory now.
I'm tired of feeling this way.
I can't depend on myself any more,
Oh, help me, Jesus, I pray.

Thank you, Lord, for hearing my prayer,
And making me depend on You.
I know that I'm still getting older,
But now my spirit is renewed.

God Loves You

I will say a prayer for you today,
Because you seem so alone.
I feel you need a special touch
That can only come from God's throne.

Did you know that God really, really loves you,
Just as much as He loves me?
He wants you to accept His love,
So your soul can be set free.

Did you know He hears a sinner's prayer,
If they ask Him to live in their heart?
And it really doesn't matter who you are,
He's loved you from the start.

He wants to share His spirit with you,
So that you can find your way;
Then you can experience all the rainbows
That He let me experience today.

I want to say a prayer for you,
Because we're all the same in God's eyes.
You don't have to pretend any more.
You know God can see through your disguise.

If you will just let Him lead the way,
You'll discover who you really are,
Because when God looks at all of us,
We all become as bright as a star.

He wants to show you a better way,
So won't you please allow Him
To become your Lord and Savior,
So that life won't look so dim?

He has a way that's not like ours,
And we can't always understand
Just what He has in mind,
But we must accept His plan.

Then we'll know Him as our savior,
And we'll trust Him all the way.
We'll never feel alone again,
Because His love is here to stay.

God's Glory

Lord, let us understand Your glory.
Teach us how to experience Your power.
Help us to find the truths we're seeking,
And come satisfied this very hour.

Help us define the words pride and satisfaction,
So we will not be afraid to speak out.
Being satisfied with our own accomplishments
Can bring victory over our fears and doubts.

Finding this satisfaction will bring peace,
And this peace will bring God's rest.
Then rest will bring us into His presence,
Where we feel worthy to be blessed.

If we will believe, as we really should,
And expect results, as He has asked us to,
There will not be anything to hold us back
From accomplishing what we need to do.

Then our eyes and ears will become ready,
And our hearts will be willing to see
That God is the one and only one
That can offer us a wisdom degree.

Grateful Friendships

We, the class, would like to thank you
For being a vessel in God's hand
And allowing Him to use you to help
All of us come to understand

That there isn't one thing as important
As trying to discover God's plan.
As we live our lives out each day,
Experiencing so many earthly demands.

We know you've allowed Him to lead you,
And give you wisdom from above.
So that you could share His Word with us,
And we could feel the warmth of His love.

We are very grateful for your friendship,
And we know you've tried your best,
To help us understand God's mysteries,
Now it's up to us to do the rest.

Yes, you have gotten us excited,
And given us a hunger to learn more.
And for that, we are so thankful.
You've helped us open one more door.

We are really going to miss you,
You've been a blessing to us all.
But we know you'll be where God needs you,
Because you have been faithful to His call.

His Plan

God places us where we will bring Him the most glory,
Even if everything in our natural life wants to run away.
It's through these experiences that we learn to trust Him,
Even if we can't find one reason that could make us want to stay.

Don't you know that He never makes one mistake?
That's why you have placed your life in His hands.
Then doesn't it make sense to release your struggle to Him?
Right now, He's the only one that could possibly understand.

Not one person that you know can change your circumstances.
Even if they wanted to help, they wouldn't have a clue.
So please don't look to man to find an answer.
Relax and let God lead. He'll get you through.

He's already given you everything you need to succeed.
You are more than qualified to get this job done.
Now offer your qualifications back to Him.
While He's using them, you just relax and have fun.

Does this seem to be taking Him for granted?
If it does, then you're finally accepting Him for who He is.
He wants you to realize that without Him, you are helpless.
And that every victory you win is really His.

So, stop right where you are and thank Him,
And tell Him you've been trying too hard to please man.
But you know that only His grace could ever be sufficient,
And then start over. But this time, use His plan.

Hope Is

Hope is expectations of good things happening in the future.
So why do so many of us choose to doubt instead?
If we will be determined in our heart to believe God's words,
Then we'll know there is no earthly reason for us to dread.

The Bible teaches us that hope deferred makes the heart sick,
But Satan wants us to believe that we can put our trust in ourselves.
That way we never get to see God's wonderful miracles,
We're too busy worrying about how to obtain health and wealth.

Hope is not just sitting around dreaming about what could be.
It's living life expecting God to teach us what is right.
And being obedient to all His wonderful commandments.
When we obey, the devil has lost the fight.

You can do anything you want to with your free will.
But how can you enjoy things you know aren't right?
What have you determined that you can never give up
Without giving God a chance to enter into sight?

Hope means that with God all things are possible.
But without hope, you are doomed to a life of woe.
Please be determined in your hearts to be obedient,
Because your blessed Savior loves each of you so.

Sure, sometimes every one of us will want to give up,
And that's when Satan will be telling his lies.
He says that you will never, never change,
And he even brings tears into your eyes.

But tell him in Jesus' name get behind me.
Because you know some day this life will end.
And you can't let him keep you from Heaven,
Because that really is when your life will begin.

I Will Be There

Ask Me anything in the world you want to,
And expect Me to answer each prayer.
Be still and listen for My voice,
And I promise you, I will be there.

But if you don't believe that I'll hear you,
Then I'm sure you are right.
Because you must truly trust that I am God,
Or you can't receive your spiritual sight

One day with me is like a lifetime.
No other one can make you feel this way.
So forget about everything that's bothering you,
And invite Me to come spend the day.

Janie

Janie, you're really a blessing to my heart.
You've been a friend, right from the start.
You're God's special work of art,
And you've really learned to live the part.

You've accepted from Him what you couldn't do.
You've allowed His peace to take hold of you.
You feel strength and become brand new,
And depend on His grace to see you through.

You give Him thanks in every way,
By experiencing His joy each and every day.
You know He will never turn you away,
Because His love is there to stay.

You accept life just like you're supposed to.
You never let that chair make you feel blue,
Because you know God knows what's best for you,
And you accept it, because you know it's true.

You are a great example to everyone,
And I truly believe you really have fun.
All of us could learn from you, Hon,
Because that's how victories are always won.

Jean

Jean, I asked God to give me a clue
On how to show my appreciation to you.
His answer to me was nothing new,
"Write her a poem, that's what you do."

So with these words I can let you know
What a special gift you have to sow.
Remember actions speak louder than dough,
So what you give makes others grow.

When you see a need, you don't run for cover,
You do it yourself, and don't ask another.
You use your strength to help your brother,
And you take charge just like a mother.

You really know how to make a house shine,
Even one as dirty and messy as mine.
I tell you, you are really one of a kind,
A more virtuous woman is hard to find.

My children rise up and call you smart,
And use words of wisdom that you impart.
You don't even realize you have an art,
In showing others how to use their heart.

I guess I'm a little jealous, you see,
Because you're what I'd like to be.
But I'm glad we both can agree,
That only God holds the true key.

I know these words are not wrong,
So some day when I become strong,
I might make this poem into a song,
So the whole world can sing along.

Johnny

Johnny, your name means "Yahweh has been gracious."
Everyone knows this definition has come true.
His Grace and Mercy have been extended to you,
And even in adversity, He keeps on blessing you.

Your road has not always been an easy one.
You've experienced your share of sickness and sorrow.
But you have never had to look back on regrets,
You just live for today, not worrying about tomorrow.

We want you to know that you are a faithful friend.
You have helped so many people who were in need.
Your wife, Ella, has been right there beside you,
Also doing such helpful and giving deeds.

Now, we ask God to send you a special blessing,
By helping you to recover and feel well again.
He needs you to keep spreading the Gospel,
So many others will become free from sin.

We're asking Him to send angels to hover over you,
And that many, many prayers will be said.
We also ask that you will feel really blessed,
While you are lying there in that hospital bed.

Thank you for all the time you have given,
And for the strength you have used for God.
Now we pray that you will be rewarded,
By His wonderful Grace that spares the rod.

Just Relax

Hi there, how are you today?
How I wish that you could answer me.
But you just being here is a miracle.
We need to thank God, don't you agree?

When I talk to you, it's like talking to God.
I know you hear, but you don't answer back.
Of course that doesn't make me love you less,
But sometimes I don't know how to act.

Should I treat you like a baby,
And talk that baby talk?
Or should I treat you like nothing happened,
And assure you one day you'll walk?

It's almost like time is standing still.
Nothing seems to change at all.
But we know God holds the future,
And He hears our desperate call.

You just relax now and talk to Jesus.
Did you know He hears you well?
So you ask Him for a miracle,
We might get it, you can never tell.

Just Think About Today

Do you worry about your future,
Instead of concentrating on today?
Or do you spend too much time thinking
About the "good 'ole yesterdays"?

Either way you are a loser,
Because now is the only time.
To put your house in order,
And to keep your family in line.

What if you did become rich and famous?
Do you think that would make things right?
Or what if you returned to the "good 'ole days"?
Do you think you'd sleep better at night?

Just think about today,
And let tomorrow take care of itself.
And let yesterday be long ago,
And put those memories on the shelf.

Kathy

Lord, thank you for our sister Kathy.
Who has truly trusted Your word.
Even though she walked through a valley,
She never doubted that You had heard.

Yes, You heard her when she felt desperate,
And You heard her through all the fear.
Because even though she sometimes doubted
She still knew that You were near.

She knew that hundreds of people were praying.
She claimed the scripture—I will live, not die.
And she knew how much You loved her,
And how You heard her when she'd cry.

So she grasped Your hand so tightly,
And she trusted You more each day.
She didn't know how You would help her,
But she knew You had a way.

Lord, thank You for our sister Kathy,
Who we look at as Your miracle child.
You brought her out of that valley,
With a spirit so meek and mild.

Krista

Krista, wipe away those tears.
Your mother is in good hands.
Jesus is watching over her,
And you must accept His plan.

He will stay right beside her.
So don't worry that you're not there.
He has everything under control,
Even the burdens she must bear.

He will give her the strength she needs
To face what the future holds.
But He has to do things His way,
Because He's the one in control.

So tell Him that you trust Him,
So that you can let go
Of all those burdens that you're carrying,
That are causing you to worry so.

God still performs many miracles.
And if that's what He has in mind,
Then all you can do is wait,
And leave those doubts you have behind.

Let Go of Bitterness

Why do we react in a negative way,
When we should take a positive view?
Why don't we accept the good and the bad,
From a God who knows what to do?

Lord, let us accept things we cannot change,
Because that is the only way
That we can keep a loving disposition,
And even want to pray.

Our prayers will not help at all
If we hold bitterness inside.
So let's turn loose of those terrible feelings,
And in our dear Lord abide.

He can change our tears into smiles,
No matter what we're going through.
If we give Him a chance to come inside,
He will change our point of view.

Mama

Mama, you're the strongest lady I know;
That's one more reason I love you so.
The Bible teaches that strength comes from above,
So Mama, you've been showered with Jesus' love.

He says He is our strength when we realize
That everything we need lies in the sky.
God is just waiting to be recognized,
When we finally decide to open our eyes.

He's the only one who can feel our pain,
And the only one to make us well again.
But there are things that we must do
To allow His spirit to really get through.

Those things don't take any earthly strength,
But like a chain we must find the length
That joins our soul to the heart of God
So Satan can't touch us with his rod.

So Mama, your strength must be really strong,
Because He has allowed you to live so long.
You've always wanted to do no wrong,
And always known to whom you belonged.

You've accepted the peace he freely gives;
I have seen that as long as I've lived.
You've given us hope all these years,
Because you always released to Him your fears.

You accepted this life just like it is
And didn't complain because you were His.
You knew somehow He'd be there for you,
So you rested in His love to see you through.

You never said you were perfect, you know,
But you were determined to never let go.
Because you knew love could hide all your sin,
So that true love you've kept within.

So one of these days when you hear His voice,
You'll be so glad that you made that choice.
He'll make you completely free from sin
And you'll never feel another pain again.

So you rest now and know you're loved,
And accept the help that comes from above.
No other one can tell you what will be
And no other soul can set you free.

So remember today as you lie in this bed
That you have no earthly reason for dread.
Because you trusted in Jesus' name
You have no reason to feel ashamed.

He took your sins to the cross with Him,
So not one soul has a right to condemn.
So today I know to whom you belong,
And now I realize who made you so strong.

Margaret

I have a special friend named Margaret,
Who is just as precious as can be.
She has so many wonderful talents,
Sometimes she really amazes me.

Today, I realized she is a great photographer.
Her pictures almost took my breath away.
They seemed to be telling a beautiful story,
Each one of them had something to say.

She and I have so very much in common.
We never run out of things to talk about.
Sometimes we have to lift each other up
Away from our feelings of worry and doubt.

I am so glad I have my friend Margaret.
She is such a blessing to me,
Especially when our prayer group prays,
And we all feel united and free.

Milly

Milly, you're a very special lady.
I bet you wonder how I know.
It isn't hard to explain at all,
Your husband told me so.

He told me you weren't feeling well,
And that you could use a lift.
And I want to say right now,
Don't you ever start to drift.

Just keep your mind on Jesus,
You know you're in His hands.
And remember all the things He's done,
And how He understands.

He's never made a mistake before,
And I'm sure He won't this time.
So when you get a little discouraged,
Just keep this poem in mind.

You are a wonderful mother and wife,
And a Christian lady as well.
You've always trusted Jesus,
So His story, you must tell.

So when you don't feel like dancing,
Or running a five mile run,
Just turn your eyes on Jesus,
And with Him, you'll have fun.

Because His joy is never ending,
And He knows just what you need.
So trust His gentle nudges,
And you will always succeed.

Mr. Harvey

Mr. Harvey, we all really miss you.
Sunday School is so much harder to do.
I'm sure that you don't have a clue,
What a terrible time we're going through.

The children need to hear you teach.
You know which souls need to be reached.
Without sounding like you're trying to preach,
Or giving them a lecture, or making a speech.

You have such words of wisdom to share,
And they listen because they know you care.
You make them happy just being there,
Yes, teachers like you are very rare.

So you hurry up and get back here,
Because your friendship is so dear.
And you being here takes away our fear,
Because you make God's Word sound so clear.

Mrs. Bibb

I know a little lady,
Mrs. Bibb is her name.
She is so sweet and friendly
And always stays the same.

We're always glad to see her
When she comes into the store.
She has such a nice smile,
And a personality we adore.

She's lost most of her hearing,
And she's afraid people will get mad.
When she can't hear what they're saying,
This make her very sad.

But, Mrs. Bibb, it doesn't matter
If you can't hear what we say.
We love to see you coming,
So don't you stay away.

Just remember Jesus loves you
And He can take away that fear.
If you listen, you will hear Him
Whisper, "I love you" in your ear.

Neighbor

I look all around me
And what do I see.
I see a lot of houses,
Each one so near to me.

Who lives in these houses,
Is something I don't know.
Because I've been so busy,
A friendship did not grow.

I feel so very guilty,
I don't even know their name.
Their faces aren't familiar,
They all just look the same.

I haven't taken the time to visit,
So I gladly take the blame.
But not knowing your neighbors
Really is a shame.

I want you to know I love you,
But I just don't know how
To be a good neighbor,
Because time will not allow.

I'd invite you to my house,
But I'm seldom there.
I have a full time job,
So there's not much time to spare.

Yes, I am a Christian.
Thank God I've been born again.
I still make plenty of mistakes,
But He forgives me again and again.

So, if you don't have a church home,
I'd love for you to go with us.
So consider yourself invited,
First Baptist on Madison is rated A+.

Open the Door

Do you have some problems
That you want to unload?
Do you have a story
That you would like told?

Do you have some guilt
That you really should let go?
Do you need a special friend
That you could really get to know?

Do you have some heartaches
That really cause you pain?
Do you have some questions
That no one can explain?

Do you ever feel alone,
Even when you're in a crowd?
Do you want to run away,
Or even cry out loud?

I had felt this very way,
So many times before.
But one day I heard my Savior,
Come knocking on my door.

Now when I feel this way,
I go to Him in prayer.
And I know I'm never alone,
Because He is always there.

You should open up the door,
And let Him come inside.
To let Him lift your burdens,
And take away that silly pride.

Peace

Have you accepted God's gift of peace today,
Or do you still experience doubt, fears and dread?
Oh how frightened we can let ourselves become,
Instead of trusting what our dear Lord has said.

He asked us not to let our hearts become troubled
And explained there is no reason to become afraid,
Because He left us His peace through the Holy Spirit,
And we can accept this peace that He freely gave.

By His peace, you can accept all life's hardships,
Because you will know they'll work out for good.
That's why we must never question the Holy Spirit,
By not reacting to our problems as we should.

By faith, we can reach out and accept it,
And by God's grace, we'll discover this wonderful peace.
If we'll just relax in the arms of our Savior,
Soon our worries, dread, and anxieties will cease.

Praise the Lord

Praise the Lord when you're crying,
Because He can wipe those tears away.
Praise the Lord when you're worrying,
He can cause those thoughts to sway.

Praise the Lord when you're feeling guilty,
He can set you free.
Praise the Lord when you're lonely,
Oh, how He can comfort thee.

Praise the Lord when you're suffering,
He can ease all the pain.
Praise the Lord when you're unhappy,
He can make you smile again.

Thank the Lord when you feel stupid,
Or you feel you've hurt a friend.
He can turn your heart to praising,
So you can feel important again.

Rearview Mirror

How do you feel about salvation?
Do you really understand the term?
Do you ever think about it,
Or do you even care to learn?

Salvation has many meanings,
But only two you have to know.
Being saved from a burning Hell,
And being able to let go.

Let go of your time,
So you won't always be looking back,
And saying, I shouldn't have done that,
And feeling guilt on your back.

Let go of that tug at your heart,
When you know you've hurt someone.
Or the time you spend thinking
Of the things you've left undone.

God can be your rearview mirror,
So you don't have to be looking back.
He can see clearly behind you,
If you'll stay on the right track.

He'll allow you to look straight ahead,
And never have to look back.
If you'll accept His calling,
He'll be everything you lack.

Ruby

I have a new friend and her name is Ruby.
I discovered quickly that she depends on the Lord.
I went to visit her to offer inspiration,
But what I received was a greater reward.

I discovered a heart that trusted the Savior,
When I entered that home that showed forth His love.
I knew immediately that I didn't need to inspire Ruby;
Her inspiration was descending from above.

She's receiving grace and mercy that only God could give her,
And accepting life one day at a time.
Yes, I thought I had come to inspire Ruby,
But I found the inspiration was really mine.

Her trust in the Savior was so very inspiring,
And her love for Him was truly strong.
Yes, I thought I had come to inspire Ruby,
But discovered to whom real inspiration belongs.

I knew He had provided everything she needed;
Because of her faith, He would see her through.
Yes, I thought I had come to inspire Ruby,
But, Lord, her inspiration comes directly from You.

She can expect miracles when Your throne she approaches,
Because by Your wisdom, she will succeed.
Yes, I thought I had come to inspire Ruby,
But I found that You would supply all her needs.

Ruth

Ruth, I've just discovered the meaning of your name,
And yes, God is the one who revealed it to me.
Jean had explained how close the two of you are,
And He has made that easier for me to see.

Ruth, your name means a female companion,
And I know that is exactly what you've been.
You have accompanied Jean on many a journey,
Yes, you've truly been a wonderful friend.

I know you were there to watch her cry,
When you knew it would break your heart in two.
So every time you stopped to wipe her eyes,
She knew she needed to wipe yours too.

But these heartaches that you both have experienced
Have provided a way for each of you to grow.
And now you two are becoming so much stronger,
As Jesus teaches you things you didn't know.

He has taught you that He will never leave you,
And that His grace will take you through.
And that you'll never get caught in the middle,
If you'll allow Him to show you what to do.

You've found He will always relieve your burdens,
Because He knows just how much you can take,
And you'll begin to feel His wonderful peace
About the time you think your heart will break.

Oh, isn't it wonderful to have a friend like Jesus,
To stand right in the middle of you two,
So that when one doesn't have the strength to speak,
The other will be there to ask Him for you.

Serenity

There is only one answer
To this dungeon I have dug.
There is only one reason,
That I deserve a big hug.

There is only one glare of light
That shines in this cell.
There is only one ray of hope,
As far as I can tell.

I know that I am not alone;
You too, have lost your way,
And landed in this dungeon.
But I pray we will not stay.

All my life, I've been searching
For happiness and fame,
And when I couldn't find it,
I almost went insane.

I knew that something was missing,
From this sin-sick heart of mine.
But it's taken so long to discover it,
I'm running out of time.

But now I see a little light,
And I'm going to start to climb
Out of this life of darkness,
And leave this sin behind.

Because someone really loves me,
And He died to set me free,
So that I can live forever,
And He will never, never leave me.

So this is my testimony,
And I hope it is yours too.
So let's all work together,
And I know that we'll pull through.

By trusting in our Father's grace,
And not ourselves alone,
He can change our sinful lives,
So we can reach His throne.

But we all must surrender
And let Him have His way.
We can't wait until tomorrow,
We must follow Him today.

Shirlon

Dear Shirlon, we want to thank you
For loving Mom the way you do.
You've spent your whole life trying
To make her happy here with you.

You can't imagine how important you've been,
You just know you love her so.
You don't seem to realize this,
That's why we needed to let you know.

Shirlon, none of us are perfect,
But we must try to understand
That we have to forgive each other,
And do the best we can.

You're Mama's little pride and joy,
And she's so proud of you.
You've really come a long way,
And she can depend on you.

Shirlon, we're all proud of you;
You and Mama are a team.
She's always wanted to stay home,
And you've provided her that dream.

She never wants to leave home,
Not even to stay with us a while.
So you must make her happy,
Because she's always kept her smile.

Stop and Listen

We've got something to tell you,
We've got something to say.
You must stop and listen,
Please don't walk away.

We've finally found the answer
To all that this life demands.
We've stopped trying to do it ourselves,
We've put it in God's hands.

Since we've let Him lead the way,
We're not afraid anymore.
We're just so excited,
He can open any door.

When we see no possible way,
His grace comes bursting through.
And then before we know it,
He shows us what to do.

Won't you trust Him with your life
And let Him lead the way?
He promises to stay close by,
And hear you when you pray.

Then you'll just have to tell others,
Because you'll have something to say.
You just can't keep it to yourselves,
Because you've found a better way.

So let's all join together,
To get this message through.
If you'll give your life to Jesus,
He'll do the rest for you.

Susan

Susan, a little birdie just told Me
That you might need a special word.
A little more than "I'm praying for you"
And a little deeper than you've heard.

Susan, you must hear Me say, "I love you,"
Through all your pain and tears.
Then you'll know I'll never leave you,
And you can release to Me your fears.

Susan, you must trust Me more now
Than you've ever done before,
So you'll be able to let go of self,
And free your mind of every chore.

Susan, I will complete the tasks for you,
If you will surrender your work to Me.
You need to take this time to rest,
To become who I want you to be.

Susan, don't try to understand Me,
Because My ways are not your way.
You must never forget I'm in charge,
And that I hear you when you pray.

Susan, I love to hear those prayers,
Every day they seem to get stronger;
But you can't expect an answer now,
You must wait a little longer.

Susan, think about things that are lovely,
And thank Me for those things.
If you will enjoy being in My presence,
You'll be ready for what the future holds.

The Real Gifts of Life

What are you thankful for today?
Please ponder before you speak.
Let your answer come from the soul,
Because all our flesh is so very weak.

Do we appreciate the real gifts of life
That come directly from God's hand?
Or do we cherish our worldly possessions,
That were made by mere man?

What in life really makes you joyous?
You will have to discover this for yourself;
Because God has given us a free will.
We all feel differently about wealth.

But today, just look all around you,
And remember this happiness we share.
And be thankful we love one another,
And for a Savior who is always there.

The Vine

You never have to be alone unless you choose to be,
Because God will dwell in a secret place with you and me.
He is the Vine and we are the branches; can't you see
That Vine produced the blood that set us free.

Without the Vine, we the branches can't survive,
To bear the fruit for which our Savior died,
So that we can share with others far and wide,
That underneath His shadow they, too, can abide.

It's really hard to always see the light,
Through the world's glasses that tend to fog our sight.
But remember faith, hope, and charity are always right,
And where they abide there is no need for fright.

And when we continue to allow them to abide,
Our precious Savior will never leave our side.
And for every problem, an answer He will provide,
All we have to do is give Him our pride.

Because you see the final victory is already won,
Jesus' work here on earth has been done.
We just have to accept Him as God's only Son,
And to allow His Vine Sap to freely run.

Then we can say, we've broken down a wall,
And through God's grace we'll never start to fall.
Now we are just waiting to hear His final call,
And to abide in Heaven will be worth it all.

Truth and Honesty

Do you happen to know someone
Who really wants to treat others right?
But he's always afraid that they won't like him,
So he exaggerates the truth to look good in their sight.

But when you try to impress your peers,
By saying words you think they want to hear,
You're always afraid they'll find you out,
And so you live your life in fear.

It also causes you to hurt your family,
Because they want to love you for who you are,
Not for trying always to impress others,
Or by having the best-kept yard or car.

They want to know that you really love them,
And hear you speak kindness in their ear.
They want to be the center of your attention,
And to be excited to have you near.

They want someone that they can depend on,
Not just someone to put food on the table,
But someone they can trust to take care of them,
So they don't feel like they're living out a fable.

Truth and honesty are a must in your life,
And if you can't offer this, you're making a big mistake,
But you can't do this by yourself,
You have to allow God to overtake.

God sees you for who you are,
And He loves you with all of His heart.
And He's not willing to give up on you,
He's just waiting for you to allow Him to do His part.

God doesn't want you to feel like you're bad.
He just wants you to keep His love within.
Then you won't be afraid of who you are on the outside.
You'll have a clear conscience, and God as your best friend.

Two Roads

Two roads lie in front of me,
Which one will I choose?
If I choose the wrong road,
Just what will I lose?

If you choose the sinful road,
God won't be your guide.
You'll have to travel all alone,
With no Savior by your side.

But look what I have to give up,
If I follow the sacred road.
I'll probably lose all my friends.
Boy, this is a heavy load.

You don't have to give up anything, son,
If you'll just follow your heart,
Because when that road ends,
Is where your new life will start.

You mean I will get to Heaven,
And see Jesus face to face?
Yes, if you follow that sacred road,
You will have won the race.

United Hearts

Thank you, Lord, for bringing all of us here,
And for allowing Your Spirit to hover so near.
Let us accept His presence, because it's clear
That Satan doesn't want us to allow Him to appear.

We really thank You for being in our midst.
Now please lead us to where answers exist,
And keep Satan from trying to twist,
All of God's truths that we must not miss.

All of us here are equal in God's eyes.
Some of us may be slow and some very wise;
But it makes no difference because we realize
That only by God's power can His Word come alive.

Now, Holy Spirit, open our minds and help us to see
That this is an opportunity to allow You to be
The only one that can make Satan flee.
Please allow our hearts to become united and free.

Let us use this time to praise Your name
And feel the joy and know why we came.
Some of us here will never be the same,
If we'll open our hearts and let Your love proclaim.

Victory

Victory! What a beautiful name for God's house!
Just saying it should make you feel free.
It's wonderful to know God has overcome the world,
It doesn't have to be won by you and me.

Aren't we glad that it's already completed,
And it didn't have to depend on us?
All we have to do is accept His righteousness,
And in His Holy Name to trust.

This victory promises us fulfillment,
By renewing our mind, so we can rest in the Lord.
We then allow Him to use us as vessels,
And we don't have to wait for eternal reward.

This victory doesn't depend on our feelings.
It's our possession because we have Christ in our heart.
So we don't have to feel that we are unworthy,
Because that victory gave us a brand new start.

So by fellowship and praise, let's comfort each other,
And always be ready to share God's Word.
Let's always be willing for Christ to use us,
Because there's so many people who still haven't heard.

Let's try and raise our standards just a little higher
And never be satisfied at the level we're on.
Let's reach our hand out just a little further;
So we can encourage others to make heaven their home.

Winner in the End

What can you lose by trusting the Lord?
You could lose a lot, my friend,
But what you lose are the things God will choose
To make you the winner in the end.

You can be set free, if you'll allow yourself,
Because He died on the cross for that freedom.
He suffered and died so you can abide.
His promises are in the Bible if you'll read them.

You're a special person in the sight of God,
I want to make this statement clear.
So the next time Satan tells you you're not,
You just quote the scripture in his ear.

If you have trouble forgiving yourself
For your past and present sins,
Just picture our Lord as He hung on the cross,
Because He settled that way back then.

You Will Win the Fight

A very nice lady came into my store
And touched my heart to the very core.
She was just as sweet as she could be,
And really seemed to enjoy talking to me.

At first, I didn't realize anything was wrong.
She looked all healthy and strong.
Then I discovered she wasn't feeling so well,
And I knew then, she had a story to tell.

The word cancer seems so hard to say,
But I was happy she shared that day,
Because it gave me a chance to pray
That if it be God's will, He'd take it away.

I can tell she still holds some fright,
But I know she also holds Jesus tight.
So I'm sure everything will turn out alright;
Together, I know they will win the fight.

Amen

Christmas, Easter & Other Special Events

Willing to Shine

The star is a symbol of the brightness of life,
And how Jesus shines forth in all His glory.
Let us examine the illumination of our hearts,
As we ponder the beautiful Christmas story.

Only one star led the Wise Men to the Christ child,
Even though all the stars were shining that night.
It was the star in the East that led them,
But they were all willing to shine their light.

There were so many, many stars in the firmament,
Some so far away, they were not even in sight.
But even though they couldn't be seen,
They were still willing to keep burning bright.

We, like the stars, are God's heavenly bodies,
And He has designed each one of us just right.
He has placed us where we are needed,
So we must be willing to shine our light.

Christmas Day

I want you to remember back, if you will,
To a lowly manger in Bethlehem.
Mary has done something no other woman could do.
She has given birth to God's only lamb.

This scene is ever etched in our hearts,
Because God had planned it that way.
He knew we would celebrate it forever,
And that we would come to call it Christmas Day.

Baby Jesus lay in that manger,
And He looked the same as any child.
But Mary and Joseph knew He was God's son,
And that they could only keep Him a little while.

Shepherds came from far away to worship Him,
Because they had seen a star in the East.
They too, knew He was the son of God,
And they came so their hearts could feast.

Wise men later came to celebrate His birth,
And they brought gifts of gold, frankincense and myrrh.
Their gifts were almost priceless,
But they couldn't compare to the gift that would occur.

When we think of this scene, what do we feel?
Does it melt our hardened hearts,
As we think of Jesus in that manger,
Does it make us want to do our part?

By helping the world to get to know Him,
From His beginning to His end,
So that they can truly come to understand,
That the only reason He was born was to die for their sin.

Christmas Story

When you think of Christmas,
What really are your thoughts?
Do you understand the real meaning
Of the peace that Jesus brought?

I am sure you know the story well,
But could I please share it again?
I feel you need a closer look
At what happened way back then.

People were going in all directions;
They could not tell right from wrong.
They were just wandering through life,
Not knowing to whom they belonged.

Oh, they had a King to rule them,
But his heart just wasn't right.
He didn't give them peace at all;
He just filled their hearts with fright.

So God looked down from Heaven
And said, "I know what you are going through.
It is time to send the Savior,
That Isaiah has promised you."

First, He sent the angel, Gabriel,
To bring the good news to earth.
By telling the Virgin Mary,
That Jesus she would birth.

She was really frightened at first,
Because she just could not understand.
How she could bear a Savior,
When she had not known a man.

But Gabriel explained that the Holy Spirit
Would cause Mary to conceive.
And that she would bear the Christ Child,
If only she would believe.

Mary knew that she was really blessed,
And her heart was filled with joy.
She had been the chosen one,
To give birth to God's baby boy.

She was betrothed to Joseph,
Who was a very godly man.
She knew that he really loved her,
But would he understand?

At first, Joseph was embarrassed;
He even thought of putting her away.
But an angel appeared unto him in a dream,
And told him everything would be okay.

He said Mary had conceived by the Holy Spirit,
And that he should not be afraid.
He must take her as his wife,
Because God's plan was laid.

He told him she would bring forth a son,
And Jesus would be His name.
And He would save His people from their sins,
And the world would never be the same.

Well, about the time Mary should deliver,
Caesar Augustus sent out a decree
That all of the world must be taxed,
And they had to go register, you see.

So Joseph loaded up the donkey,
And they started on their way.
They had to travel to Bethlehem,
Where their taxes they would pay.

After the long journey they finally arrived;
But, there was no place for them to stay.
All the rooms in the inns were taken,
Because so many had come to register that day.

But the friendly inn keeper,
Who had a heart that was right,
Told them he had a stable,
Where they could stay overnight.

Our blessed Savior was born that night,
And they wrapped Him in swaddling attire
And laid Him in a manger,
The only crib they could acquire.

Shepherds were in the same country,
Watching over their sheep that night,
When they saw the star in the East,
That filled their hearts with fright.

But an angel appeared unto them,
And brought them tidings of great joy.
The angel said, "God has sent a Savior,
In the form of a baby boy."

He told them they would find Jesus
In a manger in Bethlehem.
Then a multitude of angels came from Heaven
And were standing all around.

They sang, "Glory to God in the Highest,
Peace and Good Will Toward Men."
Then they returned again into Heaven,
After the shepherds had come to understand

That they must go and find the Christ Child,
Because they knew their words were true.
God had sent a Savior to the world,
And they wanted to worship Him too.

So they came with haste and found Him.
It was just as the angels had said.
He was lying in that manger,
With no other place to lay His head.

They could not wait to tell others
About the Miracle they had seen.
Soon the world would know about the Savior,
And how our lives He would redeem.

Mama's Christmas Love

Mama, we really love you,
And we want you to know;
You made all our Christmases special,
As we watched your face glow.

You didn't talk much about your Savior,
But we know you depended on Him,
Because He always brought you through,
Even when your future looked awfully dim.

We know that you were always thankful
For everything He did for you.
And He was always there for you,
To show you what to do.

He taught you how to sew,
So we would have clothes to wear.
And elephants and dolls for Christmas,
When there was no money to spare.

You always kept your chin up,
And never felt sorry for yourself.
Even in the hardest times,
When there wasn't much food on the shelf.

Yes, Mama, you were very special,
So we wanted everyone to see.
It was because of people just like you,
That Christmas came to be.

Christmas at Granny's

Christmas at Granny's house—
We could hardly wait.
Oh, everything looks so beautiful,
She even has Christmas plates.

Yes, Granny makes Christmas special
For each and every one,
The youngest to the oldest,
Always has such fun.

We really celebrate Jesus' birthday,
As we read about His birth.
That makes us feel warm inside,
Hearing how He came to earth.

So, in this holiday spirit,
We want to say a special thank you,
To a very special lady,
Who makes our dreams come true.

Things to Do

It's Christmas time again,
And so many thing to do,
I don't know where to begin,
I'm afraid I will never get through.

The first thing I want to do
Is to make sure my heart is right.
And remember Christmas for what it is,
My Savior was born that night.

I want to make my children happy,
And make them feel loved.
I want them to be excited,
And feel God's presence from above.

I want to help someone in need,
In some very special way,
So they can be excited,
About our Lord's birthday!

Lord, help me to depend on You,
In everything I attempt to do.
I can't do it by myself,
But together, we'll get through.

Merry Christmas, Chad

Merry Christmas, Chad, my son,
I wanted you to know
That you are very special,
And that I love you so.

Christmas is for giving.
Because God gave His son
To forgive us for our sins
No matter what we've done.

Let's celebrate this Christmas,
With love for everyone.
Let's fill our hearts with laughter,
And praise God's only Son.

He was born in a manger,
In Bethlehem long ago.
But now He is in Heaven,
Watching you as you grow.

So be happy this Christmas,
Fill your heart with cheer.
And thank our dear Savior,
For a wonderful New Year!

Celebrating Easter

When you think of Easter,
What really are your thoughts?
Do you understand the meaning
Of that Old Rugged Cross?

I'm sure you know the meaning,
But please, let me remind you again
Of how Jesus died on that tree,
So God could forgive us for our sin.

Parents, please teach your children
That celebrating Easter is so much more
Than coloring all the pretty eggs,
Or that bunny rabbit they adore.

Let them enjoy their baskets,
And the egg hunts are fun for all.
We all like dressing up,
Yes, Easter is a ball.

But the true meaning of Easter
Is more exciting than anything.
Our Savior rose from the grave that day,
And, oh, what a joy He did bring!

So let's celebrate Easter together,
And reach out to one another.
If He could forgive us for so much,
We can at least forgive each other.

The Easter Story

God sent His only son to earth,
To sacrifice His life for us.
Even though He would be cursed,
He came so men could trust.

Some people gave their hearts to Him,
While others' hearts grew cold.
Some were afraid of His powers,
And what their future might hold.

So they nailed Him on a cross,
And laughed and made fun of Him.
They didn't realize they were lost,
And without Him, their future was dim.

The soldiers that nailed Him there shouted,
"Your God does not care!
If you were really His child,
He'd make you come down from there!"

But you see, Jesus had to die.
Because that was the only way
That our sins could die with Him,
So we could be free today.

It was on a Good Friday,
That Jesus had to die,
They put Him in a new tomb,
As many watched and cried.

Sunday morning, the women came
And found the stone was rolled away.
They didn't know who to blame,
Or what had happened that day.

But suddenly two angels appeared and said,
"Tombs are for the dead;
Jesus is alive again."
Then they remembered what He had said.

"After I am risen again,
I will go before you into Galilee."
These were the words He had spoken,
So now they could clearly see.

He appeared again before many,
Before He ascended above.
They knew He had to go home,
But He had left behind His love.

Why Did He Have to Die?

I want you to go with me, if you will,
To an old rugged cross on Golgotha Hill.
Now picture our Lord, His body so still.
He died for you, friend; this scene is real.

They said He had lied, that He wasn't God's son.
They laughed and they scorned and made fun.
They didn't flinch as they watched His blood run.
They thought He had lost, and they had won.

They never believed His words were true.
They didn't want Him telling them what to do.
They thought He was a man, just the same as you
And they didn't care what He was going through.

Now go with me to the tomb where His body lay,
And watch as the stone rolled away.
God had no intentions of letting Him stay.
So Jesus rose on the third day.

Why did He have to die for you and me?
So He could forgive our sins and set us free.
Yes, now we can live victoriously,
By becoming who He wants us to be.

Salvation

My Jesus' love came softly,
As You crept into my heart.
I know my life had finally changed,
And we would never part.

I didn't understand at first,
But now I truly see
That He had taken over,
And He'd take care of me.

I know I had to accept His ways,
That I really didn't understand.
I now know I answer to God,
And never again to man.

He has shown me many mysteries,
As I daily read the Word.
And He whispers words of wisdom
That the world has never heard.

I know that He can hear me,
So there's no reason not to pray;
And I know He's always there,
Even when He seems so far away.

Yes, Jesus' love came softly,
And I want the world to see
That even though they'll still make mistakes,
Their souls can be set free.

Mother's Day

Today, I lift up every mother,
On their very special day.
Lord, I ask You to lead and guide them,
Because without You, they will stray.

A mother has an awesome responsibility
Of bringing up a child today.
They have to have Your patience, Lord,
So by Your side, they must stay.

They must put their own life on hold,
Because of all the time it takes,
And they can never depend on self,
That would really be a big mistake.

They also need Your strength, Lord,
Without it, they will surely fall
Under all the daily pressures,
Of trying to satisfy every call.

So reach down and touch each mother,
And let them know You'll lead the way,
So that they can be a wonderful mother,
But they must remember to take time to pray.

My Valentine

Will you be my valentine?
He whispers in your ear.
Will you always love me,
Without reservation or fear?

Will you let me care for you,
In sickness and in health?
Will you let me provide for you,
From my Father's wealth?

Will you accept the gifts
That I've prepared for you?
Will you always trust me
To make your dreams come true?

Will you let me build us a house,
With a foundation so strong?
Then no storm can touch us,
No matter what goes on.

Will you stay close beside me
All the rest of your days?
Will you try to understand me?
And accept all my ways?

Also, you must put me first.
I'm quite jealous, you see.
I couldn't bear to think
That you'd love anything more than me.

But I'll always give you freedom.
I've trusted you from the start.
I'll be kind and compassionate.
I do have a tender heart.

I promise to always forgive you,
No matter what you do.
You must always say you're sorry,
But I'll never condemn you.

Will you be my valentine?
I know we'll have such fun.
Please say you will, my beloved,
So the two of us can become one.

Congratulations, Liz

Liz, I felt that I would like to honor you,
By expressing a few words to inspire.
I feel you truly need to be recognized,
As a lady who has accomplished her desires.

You have been a very ambitious daughter,
And have reached so many of your goals.
For this you should be proud of yourself,
But it seems now the biggest one unfolds.

You have met the man of your dreams,
And you will soon become husband and wife.
He will be able to share all your desires,
As you both begin to make a new life.

Your parents have always been there for you.
Now they are excited about your chosen mate.
God has truly hand picked your husband,
Because you've been patient enough to wait.

Robert, I want to congratulate you too,
And wish you the very best in life.
You have really gotten started the right way,
By deciding to pick Liz for your wife.

Now both of you must always remember,
You have to put God before each other.
If you keep Him the center of your household,
You can't help but love one another.

ENGAGEMENT

My little girl has gotten engaged.
How am I supposed to feel, my dear?
I guess I knew someday it would happen,
But now that day is really here.

You know, all I want is your happiness,
And for you to keep God first in your life.
Love and obey your husband, darling,
Oh! I know you'll be a good wife.

You're going to be such a beautiful bride,
And the groom will look handsome too.
I know you both will be so happy,
Oh! I'm so very proud of you.

Things have not always been this easy.
I know you've had your share of strife.
But thank God your past is behind you,
And look ahead to a wonderful life.

Remember, you'll still be my little girl,
And I want you to know I'll always be here.
You'll never outgrow your need for Mom.
Now I will have both of you to hold dear.

Maybe one day you will surprise me
With a darling little grandchild.
But I think I'm running ahead of myself,
That may not happen for quite a while.

Anyway, my darling, you know I love you.
And I want you to be as happy as can be.
I know your home will be a little haven,
But you better not forget to visit me.

Leigh's Blessing

Leigh, you're a very special daughter of God.
He has your name written in the palm of His hand.
You've been a blessing to Him every day of your life,
Because you have chosen to always live by His plan.

You have also remembered to put others first,
And you've chosen to be patient, kind, and true.
You have truly learned how to wait on the Lord.
You have expected Him to always see you through.

I look at you now and see a dream coming true,
One that you patiently waited for so very long.
That perfect mate that God had promised you
Is finally here, and soon to you, he will belong.

Leigh, that is because God picked him for you,
And you know for sure God makes no mistakes.
So very soon, you two will come together as one,
And you will finally have the icing on your cake.

You know God intended for you two to meet.
Someone who would be there to hold your hand.
So Hank, God has put Leigh's hand into yours.
You have been chosen to be that very special man.

Yes, God has truly brought you two together.
Now, you must remember to put Him above all.
Allow Him to take His place as head of the home.
If not, the house could crumble and fall.

Leigh, I know you will be such a beautiful bride.
And Hank, you must really be a wonderful man,
To have won the heart of God and Leigh,
By becoming the man worthy of her hand.

May God bless you and always prosper you,
With good health, happiness, and a very long life.
Hank, always be the very best husband you can.
And Leigh, be a loving and obedient wife.

My Baby Boy Is Getting Married

My baby boy is getting married,
How am I supposed to feel?
You know all I want is his happiness;
But will he be my baby boy still?

He's always been my pride and joy,
And you know I've loved him so.
Will she take his love from me,
Or will she cause his love to grow?

He needs someone to take care of him,
Like I've always tried to do.
And someone who'll be patient;
Oh, Lord, they both need You.

I truly believe she loves him, Lord,
And I know he loves her too.
So I guess I have to turn him loose,
And, Lord, the rest is up to You.

I've taught him all about You, Lord,
And I prayed for him every night.
So now I'm ready to release him
Into the arms of his beautiful wife.

Lord, she really is a lovely girl.
Let me accept her as my own.
She's a part of the family now,
And I pray she'll always feel at home

Wendy

Oh! Wendy, I'm so happy for you!
You've chosen your companion for life.
He must really be a special person,
Because you've agreed to be his wife.

I know you will have a wonderful marriage,
Because both of you trust in the Lord.
You must always depend upon His wisdom,
And you will reap all His rewards.

Your future holds many mysteries,
But you must live only for today.
Because if you start worrying about tomorrow,
You will take all of today's joys away.

Just live each day to its fullest,
And don't ever let time pass you by.
Remember never get caught in the clouds,
Or you might miss the clear blue sky.

God will make your dreams come true,
But never forget to give Him the glory.
And you must always put Him first,
Because He's the author of life's story.

So, congratulations and best wishes.
You're everything your mom has prayed for.
You're godly, gifted, and beautiful.
Bryan couldn't ask for anything more.

Wesley and Trish

I wish you the very best in your marriage,
May all your plans and dreams come true.
I'm so glad you're best friends first,
Because friendship, as well as love, is needed too.

But you'll need the most important friend of all,
And that's Jesus by your side.
If you will always accept His ways,
Neither of you will have anything to hide.

May God grant you all your desires,
As you let His love shine through.
And may He always rule your home,
As He teaches you what to do.

May you and your sweet little family
Make Him the most important part,
Because without Him, it'll never be complete.
So welcome Him from the very start.

May this marriage be made in Heaven,
And never let the world get in the way,
Because it doesn't have anything to offer,
No matter what others may say.

So, congratulations, Wesley and Trish.
Let us know if there's anything we can do.
Remember we'll be praying
That your love will stay fresh and new.

Proud Parents to Be

To Billy and Dawn, the proud parents to be,
I'd like to express what you mean to me.

Billy, you are a special gift from above,
That God sent to all our family to love.

Dawn, you were born when I needed you so,
To help me in a time I needed to grow.

You've been there for me all of these years,
Sometimes through a whole lot of fears.

But today, the world looks so bright,
As we wait for this baby to come into sight.

I pray you will both put your faith in God,
While you're learning how not to spare the rod.

I know you have waited a very long time,
And that there have been mountains to climb.

But see how faithful God has been all along,
He has caused your love to become so strong,

Now that you are ready to share that love,
With this precious baby He has sent from above.

Jaden Shelby Wall

Jaden Shelby Wall, you are truly a gift from God.
We couldn't have asked for anything more.
You're as lovely as a morning star,
And as precious as any baby ever before.

We've been waiting a long time for your entrance,
But your mommy never doubted it at all.
She trusted God that when He was ready,
He'd deliver her a little baby Wall.

She knows that God will love and nurture you,
And that you will grow up loving Him.
Because she and your daddy know Him personally,
And they both know how much He loves them.

We pray that you will grow healthy and strong,
And that your life will be a blessing to all.
We also pray that you will always depend on God,
Because without Him, we all would surely fall.

Dear God, we thank You for baby Jaden,
We want to dedicate her life to You today.
We promise we will never come between you
And the choices that will show her You're the way.

Emma

A prayer is answered, Emma is here,
This baby girl that we hold dear.
A gift from God, alive and well,
A future not one soul can tell.

But to the present we happily grasp,
This dear child who's here at last.
Amazed by such miraculous charm,
Our aim in life to keep from harm

But with great determination and a little dread,
We humbly pause and bow our head.
We know her future is in God's hands,
And can never be altered by our demands.

So God, we offer her back to You,
To keep her safe and see her through.
We pray that you will always be our guide,
And that we will never give way to pride.

We gladly recognize You as Dad,
And with humble hearts we feel so glad,
That we have a Father such as You,
To guide this child her whole life through.

Hayden

Welcome to God's world, Hayden.
We are all so excited you are here.
You are everything we had hoped for.
You are so precious and so dear.

You are such a handsome boy,
And we already love you so.
We're excited about your future,
And a chance to watch you grow.

Hayden, remember Jesus loves you,
And He will always be close by.
You don't ever have to be afraid,
He hears you every time you cry.

Mommy and Daddy really love you,
And big sister, Emma, loves you too.
Mee-mee and Paw-paw plan to spoil you,
And try to make your dreams come true.

God, thank You for this precious child,
That was born to us this day.
We dedicate him to You, Lord,
May he never walk away.

Baby Boy

This beautiful son I give to you,
To cherish and to raise;
And all I ask of you in return
Is your thanksgiving and your praise.

Bring him to Me and offer him up,
And I will direct his ways,
And all I ask of you in return
Is your thanksgiving and your praise.

I will love him even more than you,
And stay with him throughout his days,
And all I ask of you in return
Is your thanksgiving and your praise.

Look to Me for the wisdom you need
And with My miracles you'll be amazed,
And all I ask of you in return
Is your thanksgiving and your praise.

You must teach him to obey Me,
So that when into his eyes you gaze,
You'll see My face staring back at you,
Then I'll know you've given Me praise.

Baby Girl

A baby girl, a gift from God,
An answered prayer, a precious pod
That opened up just in time,
With perfect health and perfect mind.

A face of beauty, God's special mold,
Awaiting a story soon to be told.
Never to be altered by other hands,
A work He started; He'll complete His plan.

You must guide her as she starts to grow,
But turn her loose into hands that know.
His perfect will He must impart,
To mold this child from the very start.

Be patient always and don't complain,
Because your life will never be the same.
But if you'll allow Him to take the lead,
Your child will grow and always succeed.

Happy Birthday, Evelyn

Evelyn, a little birdie told me it's your birthday,
And that you might enjoy hearing a little rhyme.
So I told them that if the Lord directed me,
I would gladly take the time.

I hear you're eighty years old today,
And still as bright and active as ever.
I also know that you're really involved with your church,
And always ready for any new endeavor.

It's exciting for me to see someone your age,
Still taking such an active part.
This world needs more women like you,
Who have a sincere and willing heart.

I also hear you're one of the best mothers around.
I know your children really feel blessed.
You've taught them to love and feel loved,
And released them to Jesus to teach them the rest.

I sincerely hope you're having a wonderful day,
And that all your dreams are coming true.
You personally know who can make this happen,
So just ask and watch what He'll do.

Staying active is so very important,
Because there are things only you can do.
Age just brings more wisdom for helping,
Because of all the times God's seen you through.

So, Evelyn, you just keep on keeping on.
After all, eighty is not really that old.
You've still got a lot of good years left,
To help get God's story told.

Mrs. Constance

Mrs. Constance, we want to sincerely thank you
For allowing God to use your point of view.
By using Explorer's Bible Study the way you do,
To make His Word become fresh and new.

We at Clarksville, TN, want to send our love
To a person who looks to only God above,
In order that she can give us a shove,
In uncovering mysteries the Bible is full of.

We hear that you're having a special birthday,
And we wanted to bless you in some little way.
So we're sending you a big "Hip, Hip, Hooray,"
That will make you smile and feel young and gay.

You'll be in our prayers, we want you to know,
As each one of us here continues to grow.
Because of the precious seed that you sow,
Our lives become richer as we feel His blood flow.

Mary's Best Wishes

Our dearest Brother and Sister Lee,
You've meant so much to W. J. and me.
You've helped us to open our eyes to see
Just how wonderful salvation can be.

You've shared your time when we needed you,
And given us encouraging words when we were blue.
You've shown us that dreams do come true,
And you've watched as God has pulled us through.

We thank you from the bottom of our hearts
For showing us how to find a new start.
And how to dodge Satan's fiery darts,
By seeking God's grace that He gladly imparts.

But today is your day to be blessed,
So we want to join in with all the rest
To make your day a big success
On this, your fiftieth year of marital fest!

We hope you'll celebrate many more,
And cherish each one as never before.
Your time together, don't ever ignore,
God has put you together to love and adore.

Graduation

So, you're finally graduating,
How does this make you feel?
Are you excited about the future?
Or are you just dreading the ordeal?

Maybe you're feeling a little frightened,
About the choices you're having to make?
Now that you're dealing with decisions
That others used to undertake.

If you're going away to college,
You may be dreading being alone
And leaving your friends and families,
And the security of your home.

Or, maybe you've chosen to stay at home,
And attend a college nearby.
And now you're wishing you were leaving,
And you're asking yourself why.

Maybe some of you have chosen the work field,
Because you think you need a school break.
But the more you think about it,
You're afraid you've made a mistake.

I know all of you would like an answer
To all these questions in your heart.
But only time will tell
Whether you've made the right start.

But if you've decided to go far away,
Or just stay right here at home,
You'll always have one person with you,
And He will never leave you alone.

If you will let the Holy Spirit direct you,
He will never let you down,
Because He has all the right answers
That will turn your mistakes around.

So please, don't worry or fret
About what the future holds,
Trust in God and it will turn out right,
And a successful person He will mold.

Jeremy

Oh Jeremy, how we love you!
It must be plain to see
That you're the apple of our eye.
You're the son we knew you'd be.

We know you've had to struggle,
To get to where you are today.
But God was always with you,
Because you knew how to pray.

Sometimes things seemed impossible,
But you just kept pressing on.
I'm sure we pressed too hard sometimes,
When you needed to be left alone.

But we made it through, didn't we?
Now I know you'll reach the top.
With that diploma in your hand,
"Ole opportunity" is going to knock.

And when you hear it knocking,
And you're so excited you could burst,
Don't you ever open up that door,
Until you talk to Jesus first.

Because He has all the answers,
And He's brought you safe thus far.
He'll always be there for you,
No matter where you are.

So now your graduation day is here,
And you've finally become a man.
Now you take that diploma with pride,
When they place it in your hand.

And know we are so proud of you,
Because you've proved yourself once more.
Now you're really getting closer
To opening up that door.

God Speed

Chuck and Mickey, we just wanted to let you know
Just how special you are, before we let you go.
You've been an inspiration to all of us here,
And it's been such a blessing having you so near.

That's why it would be impossible to say good-bye,
So we're saying, "God speed" and we won't even try.
We're all a little envious, but trying not to let it show.
We too would like that freedom of just letting go.

And to experience that peace that retirement brings,
And having the liberty of doing our own thing.
We know you'll have no trouble making new friends,
But you'll never be so far away that our friendships will end.

So remember as your new journey starts,
That you will always remain in our hearts.
We hope that all your dreams will come true,
But please, don't forget how much we love you.

H.R. Wortham

H.R. Wortham is a name of renown.
People know him all over this town.
He has always been a giving man,
Willing to help and to understand.

Food Town will never be the same
Without Wortham before the name.
He's devoted his life to that store.
It will never be the same anymore.

He's also been devoted to the Lord.
One day he'll receive his award
For being the husband, father, and friend
That most men can only wish they'd been.

He's worked hard for all these years.
Now we would like to give a cheer,
And wish him nothing but the best.
He's finished the work and passed the test.

Now he can sit back and relax,
And not have to worry about income tax.
He can enjoy life and just feel free,
As he sits in his chair watching T.V.

My Retirement

Winn Dixie employees, you are the best,
And I'm glad I did my part.
But now it's time to move in a new direction,
Where I might help to change another's heart.

I won't say goodbye to you all,
Because I'll still be in the neighborhood.
So anyone is welcome to come by.
I'd really appreciate it if you would.

I wish that you didn't have to work so hard,
And feel so much anxiety and stress.
I don't miss that part at all,
I really must confess.

Well, I still have some bridges to cross,
And my future definitely isn't clear.
But I know God is on my side,
So He's taking away my fear.

So I just wanted to say I love you,
The way I do it best;
By writing a poem to express,
By knowing you, I've been blessed.

Moms in Touch

Have you ever heard of "Moms in Touch"?
If not, you really must hear.
These moms are praying for your children,
Throughout the whole school year.

They meet together every week,
And talk to God about them.
Believe me, things start happening,
When they bring their problems to Him.

He appreciates this effort they give,
To make a difference in their child's school.
They even pray for changes,
If things are happening against God's rule.

But no matter how big the problem,
They know that God's big enough
To stop the devil from winning,
When the battle is getting rough.

Do you have a school aged child?
If so, you too should pray
That you can be a mom in touch,
And God will show you the way.

It's really very simple,
The only requirement is trusting God.
And you may save some child from hurting,
Or the chastening of God's rod.

God's Message to Clarksvillians

City of Clarksville, please hear My voice.
Don't let your city to be destroyed for naught,
Nor your lives saved without reason.
Accept with conviction what this storm has brought.

Nothing happens that My hand doesn't manifest.
I clearly see what each heart contains.
Search out what you are personally allowing,
That you know without a doubt should be changed.

Don't try to search for My reasoning,
Because My ways are past finding out.
Just accept that I am God, your creator.
After this, how could any of you still doubt?

I, and only I, have all the answers,
That some of you thought you had.
You have been trying to live your life your way,
Not even realizing that your ways are bad.

Open your eyes and look all around you.
Why did this destruction have to be?
Why couldn't you have just loved and trusted Me?
Don't you realize that Jesus is the key?

I've given you a way to live Holy,
By allowing My Son to take away your sins,
But so many of you haven't accepted Him personally;
And you're still putting your trust in men.

Please accept this disaster as a blessing,
That was sent as a message of hope and love.
You must repent of your heartless actions,
And accept My eternal gift from above.

God's New House

The campaign has ended,
The victory has been won.
But is the struggle over,
Or has it just begun?

Faith is the only answer,
We've known that from the start.
Prayer can take us to the throne,
But we must do our part.

The challenge has been exciting,
And the fellowship's been great.
We all pulled together,
And we've left no room for debate.

Because God knew what He was doing,
When He stated His demand.
He knew we needed a bigger building,
And He'd carry out His plan.

But we have to remain faithful,
As we open up our hearts
And allow Him to fill us,
As we try to do our part.

Yes, the Victory is His alone,
And He deserves all the glory.
Let's remember who made this happen,
When we're telling our Victory Story.

Are we all that we can be?
Or must we continue to search?
Even with our beautiful new building,
We, the people, are still God's church.

Parting Words for Family & Friends

It's Hard to Say Good-bye

It is really hard to say goodbye
To someone you love so dear.
It is even harder to imagine
How you will live without them here.

It seems your heart will break,
And the pain will never end.
You feel like part of you is gone,
Because you have lost your best friend.

You cannot think about tomorrow,
Because your grief has hold of you.
All you want is for the day to pass,
And wonder how you will ever get through.

But God has not left, you know.
He promised always to be there.
When you think you cannot go on,
Then you must go to Him in prayer.

See, He knows why this happened.
His reasoning is clear to Him.
He knew it was time to take them,
And His way, we cannot condemn.

He never makes one single mistake,
So we must know He had a plan
To make their life begin in Heaven,
As He took them by the hand.

Why don't you ask God to help you?
Realize this awful burden you hold.
He can take away your sorrow
And bring peace into your soul.

Your loved one cannot come to you,
But you can go to them someday.
If your soul belongs to Jesus,
He will show you the way.

Soon your heart will be mended,
And your life will go on.
Because God promised us victory,
And He will never leave you alone.

Charlene

Charlene, you were not only the oldest,
But the smartest from our family of six.
None of us ever had a problem
That you didn't think you could fix.

You were strong willed and very direct,
When you thought we had a need.
You always had to be the leader,
Because you wanted to help us succeed.

We all dearly loved you
And every one of us agree
That you were the big sister that felt responsible
For who we would turn out to be.

You always loved to give us presents,
Whether it was something old or something new.
It didn't matter what they were,
It was just your way of saying, "I love you."

You were definitely the strongest;
You proved that all these years.
And you were the bravest by far,
You never once gave in to fears.

You could even still out-talk us
When your voice box was gone.
We were so proud of how you handled that;
You proved that you were strong.

We pray you are in heaven now,
Still watching out for all of us,
Where you will never have to feel lonely,
Or listen to anyone fuss.

You can live the dreams you dreamed,
And be free from every pain.
We are so thankful that you're at peace,
But *our* lives won't be the same.

We will miss you so very much,
But one day we'll be together above,
Where we can just sit at Jesus' feet,
As he pours out His sweet love.

Mark

Mark, I need to write you a poem, but where do I start?
How do you write a poem, with a broken heart?
We've loved you since birth; you were so special and smart,
And we are so saddened that you had to depart.

But I know you are in heaven; God has assured me
That you are there with Him, just as content as can be.
I guess you just needed to be set free,
So He took you home, to live eternally.

Mark, ask God to give all of us here His grace;
Until the day we too can see His face.
You know that our love for you will never be erased,
But we must be willing to finish our race.

Through God's strength, and none of our own,
We will depend on His love, until He calls us home.
And then we will all be together, no more to roam.
We'll be one big family around our Father's throne.

Jack

We, the family, have a few words to say
On this very sad Memorial Day.

We felt everyone should understand
That Jack Nunn was an honorable man.

He honored God right from the start
By accepting Him personally into his heart.

He honored his father and mother, no doubt,
As he and his five brothers worked hard to help out.

Then he honored his country and with great joy
He enlisted in the Army when only a boy.

He met and married a virtuous woman one day
And has honored her in every way.

He honored his two boys that God gave him
By trying to direct and provide for them.

He honored his church by taking an active part
And every task he attempted came from his heart.

He honored his friends by being a friend.
To his entertaining and sharing there was no end.

Now we, the family, would like to give back
By expressing to you just some of the facts.

Because when it comes to being an honorable man,
He definitely has drawn his line in the sand.

Kate

Dear Kate, we would like to honor you,
As we gather here to say goodbye.
You were a lady that obeyed God's Word,
So you didn't have to be afraid to die.

We know you had a great homecoming,
With all the saints that have gone on before.
And now you're having a great reunion,
Walking along God's beautiful shore.

You have acquired what we're all striving for:
A release from this world of sin.
No more sickness, disappointment, or dread,
A deliverance from self and men.

So Kate, we don't have to grieve today,
Our hearts can actually feel light.
Your battles on this earth have ended,
You'll never see another dark night.

You were our teacher, our parent, our friend,
But you allowed everyone to lead their own lives.
You were careful never to interfere,
Especially with your stepsons and their wives.

You taught school for thirty-six years,
And that alone deserves a hand.
Love, patience, kindness, and endurance
Were only a few of your demands.

You could always enter a conversation.
And because you were so well read,
You would always have an input,
No matter what was being said.

We'll always remember your great cooking,
I'm sure most here have tasted some treat
That you prepared with such talent,
That we could hardly wait to eat.

You had so many talents besides cooking.
I could never mention them all.
Politics, gardening, literature, bridge,
And, oh yes, you dearly loved football.

Your favorite book was the Bible
And you read it as long as you could see.
I'll always remember reading it to you,
And how you dearly loved to hear me.

Aunt Lou

Dear Aunt Lou, oh, how we all loved you.
You treated us like we were your very own.
And everyone in the family really knew
That we were always welcome in your home.

Most aunts never kept in touch like you did.
At Christmas, we'd receive a gift we would adore.
Your many, many talents were never hid,
Because those gifts weren't bought from a store.

You always seemed so proud of us all.
I never heard you put any of us down.
Sooner or later, you'd give us a call,
To make sure we were safe and sound.

You loved it when we all visited you.
You'd always fix us a special treat.
Those homemade cookies were good too.
You always enjoyed seeing us eat.

You loved taking pictures of everyone.
And you treated each one like a treasure.
At the time we didn't think it was fun,
But now we realize, it was our pleasure.

Aunt Lou, you made us feel loved,
And we're really going to miss you.
But I know in your new home above,
That they're proud to have your love too.

Uncle Joe

Uncle Joe, you would be so proud of us,
As we gather here to say good-bye.
I can hear you saying now,
I want you to rejoice instead of cry.

You know you had lived a long life,
And it was time to meet your Lord.
To see the place He had prepared for you,
Where you will be not only loved, but adored.

Yes, you were loved here by many
Friends, family, and everyone you met,
Because you were the type of guy,
That people wouldn't easily forget.

I remember before I became a Winn,
How you made me feel so much a part
Of the family that I couldn't wait to join,
That had such wonderful hearts.

You always made us feel so welcome,
With a hug or a great big kiss.
Yes, that is just a small part,
Of what everyone here will miss.

We remember how you loved to play golf,
Especially with one of your many sons.
You always seemed to enjoy yourself,
And wanted everyone around you to have fun.

We know you missed Aunt Lillian,
Yes, she truly was your heart.
You always kept those vows you took,
Until death do us part.

I hope you two are united again,
And reminiscing about those days.
With the angels playing beautiful music,
As you sit at God's feet and praise.

I pray we will all be a family there,
Where there won't be so much strife,
And we will, if we have accepted Jesus,
Because He promised us everlasting life.

Ann

Our dear friend has gone to be with the Lord.
She was such a wonderful mother and wife.
This has been such a shock to us all,
Because she had been living such a radiant life.

Her love for others made her a showcase,
That would cause her to stand out more than most,
Because her smile let you know that she was sincere,
Although she was never one to boast.

Her children can rise up and call her blessed,
Because they knew she loved them with all her heart.
Her husband feels honored that the Lord blessed him
With a wife that was willing to do her part.

Being a teacher gave her a chance to reach out,
To touch so many with her wisdom and understanding.
She was never too busy to offer advice,
To influence a life without being too demanding.

She was a special, caring child of God,
And she always knew the right words to say.
That's why I think it's such an awesome honor
To be expressing my feelings in words, here today.

So, I'd like to tell everyone in this room,
That we've all experienced a great loss;
But heaven's doors have been opened wide
To a wonderful friend who bore her cross.

Aunt Elizabeth

Aunt Elizabeth, you will really be missed.
Your help didn't go unnoticed, you know.
Everyone in the family would depend on you,
Especially when our finances were getting too low.

You trusted us like we were your own,
And you were always at the big family dinners.
Even though you had a lot of health problems,
You'd even come in the dead of winter.

You were a good wife to Uncle Tom,
And we know you loved him so.
Now you can be together in heaven,
We wish we were there to see you glow.

We'd like to thank you for all you've done,
As we say good-bye for the last time here.
We'd also like to give you a hand of applause,
Because your love and fellowship was so dear.

Cookie

Cookie, your name truly describes you,
Sweet, enjoyable and good.
No name could have been better,
Or been better understood.

You were such an inspiration,
To every person you've met.
You will never be forgotten,
You're impossible to forget.

You blessed so many people.
You always stayed the same.
Your prayers were so beautiful,
As you prayed in Jesus' name.

Goodness and mercy followed you,
Each and every day.
No matter what your circumstances,
You never walked away.

You always seemed to have fun,
And you never lost your smile.
You touched so many people,
By your beautiful lifestyle.

You were almost like a magnet,
As you drew people to your side.
And your life was an open book,
You had nothing at all to hide.

Your husband, children, and grandchildren
Were very blessed to be a part
Of your wonderful family,
That you loved with all your heart.

You really knew how to live,
And you were never afraid to die.
You gave God His rightful place,
And you never had to ask why.

You have left behind a great legacy,
That most of us only dream of.
You were a perfect example,
Of how to walk in love.

Cookie, you're going to be missed,
But we all know where you are.
You're at home with Jesus,
Your bright and morning star.

There's no better place to be
Nor, no other place so sweet.
I can just see you now,
As you worship at His feet.

We, fellow prayer warriors, thank you,
And recognize all you've done.
Many people have received answers,
And many souls have been won.

Plan a Reunion

Lesa, Dan, Melanie, Joseph, and Jessica,
Bring your burden to the Lord.
He's the only one who can bear it,
That's why He's worshipped and adored.

He will never leave your side,
Or be angry when you ask Him why,
Because He knows how much you're hurting,
And He hates to hear you cry.

God's ways are not like ours,
And we can't always understand
Why bad things have to happen
For Him to work out His heavenly plan.

But Daniel didn't take his life,
His life wasn't his to take.
He had already given it to Jesus,
And he's forgiven for Christ's sake.

Because one thing we know for sure,
Christ died to set us free.
How could He love us more?
He gave His life for you and me.

Soon our lives on earth will end,
Every one of us will surely die.
But the place He has prepared for us
Hasn't any clouds in the sky.

There will be no more crying there,
And no one carrying any shame.
No more sin or sorrow,
Or wondering who is to blame.

Think about that wonderful home
That Daniel has gone to.
And ask him to plan a reunion,
For all his friends and you.

Mommy and Daddy

Mommy and Daddy, please don't cry.
No, you must not grieve for me.
Be happy and live life to the fullest.
You gave me life, don't you see?

So that Jesus could take me to be with Him,
Where my new life can never end.
I now have a beautiful home in heaven,
And some day you will see me again.

You gave me everything that I needed.
You did the best you possibly could.
Thank you for being my parents.
You both are so kind and so good.

I know you have so many questions,
And that you wanted to raise me there.
But Jesus had a bigger purpose for me,
And now I'm in His glorious care.

Jesus has a purpose for you too,
So don't worry about what you can't see
Just finish the tasks that He gives you
Then you can go to heaven like me.

Sweet Mother

In memory of my sweet mother,
These words I've chosen to say,
"Mom, you were the very best and
You proved it in every way."

You were loving and forgiving,
And everyone was your friend.
You never once stopped giving,
You were busy up to the end.

I would like to tell the world,
That it has experienced a great loss,
But Heaven's doors have been opened wide,
To a mother who bore her cross.

Sweet Memories

My mother left this earth today,
And it was so hard to say good-bye.
But I know she is in heaven,
So Lord, why do I cry?

She spent her life just trying,
To make all our dreams come true.
So Lord, now she can experience rest,
As she lives in peace with You.

She left behind sweet memories,
Of things she's said and done.
And she will never be forgotten,
But her race she's finally won.

As I Remember Mother

As I sat there by your bedside,
Knowing that you were leaving me,
I felt that I just couldn't let go,
Even though I knew you must be free.

I thought about the good times we had,
And how much you had loved us all.
I realized that it was time to say goodbye,
Because you had heard your heavenly call.

You thanked me for what I'd done,
When I knew you had done the most
By making our family what it is,
But never once did you boast.

You just accepted life, one day at a time,
And did the best you could each day.
I remember you as being a faithful
And loving mother in every way.

I know I must turn you loose now,
Knowing that you are at peace,
But I'm the one who should thank you, Mother,
For memories that will never cease.

Breathe a Prayer

When you start to grieve for me,
Just breathe a simple prayer.
Ask God to fill your heart,
And make you become aware,

That I am where He wants me,
And it's such a lovely place.
He knew my work there was over,
And that I had finished the race.

So, please be happy for me,
One day, you can be here too.
If you've accepted Jesus as your Savior,
Because that's *all* you have to do.

Don't Cry for Me

Don't cry for me, my darling.
No, you must not grieve for me.
We had a wonderful life together,
I know, with this, you will agree.

We laughed, we cried, we did it all,
But now, it's time to say our good-byes.
You must start a new life, darling.
So I want you to dry your eyes.

Be happy, and live life to the fullest.
Don't worry at all about me.
I'm just as alive as you are.
In a beautiful place you can't see.

But, one day, we'll meet again,
And then you will understand.
That life, where I am, is wonderful.
It's Canaan's promised land.

Letting Go

Why is it so hard to let you go?
It must be selfish of me
To want so much to have you back
When I know you're finally free.

You were ready to leave this earth,
And to make your home up above.
But it isn't easy to say good-bye
To someone you dearly love.

You were all any wife could want,
You took care of me in every way.
It's so hard to turn you loose,
And it gets harder every day.

But your memory will never leave me,
This promise I make to you.
You will never be forgotten, dear,
Your memories will carry me through.

I Can't Let Go

I see your smile.
I hear you speak.
I can't let go,
I am too weak.

You were the best.
You touched my heart.
I'd hoped we'd never
Have to part.

You changed my life.
You made me whole.
I loved you so.
You touched my soul.

Good-bye, my love,
I set you free,
But I'll never let go
Of your sweet memory.

My Dearest Wife

I truly respect with all my heart,
This wife, who has left behind
So many, many broken hearts.
One of them, being mine.

She was more than I could ask for.
She made me feel complete
And she will truly be missed.
Her presence was so sweet.

But I know God's arms were open,
When she walked through the heavenly gate,
And one day, He'll welcome me too.
But for now, I'll have to wait.

So goodbye, my dearest wife,
I'm thankful for all you did,
The memories will stay with me forever,
Even when the grief is hid.

Loving Husband

You were everything I could have hoped for.
You made all my dreams come true,
I couldn't have asked for a better husband.
Now only memories will carry me through.

God allowed us to be together for a reason,
But in His wisdom, He knew it was time
For you to spend the rest of your life with Him,
But I must stay here for Him to lead mine.

Now when I feel deserted and lonely;
And start to question why you had to go,
I'll remember how much He loves you,
And then my faith will start to grow.

I realize He never makes one mistake.
He knew it was time for you to leave.
So He took you into His loving arms.
Lord, remind me of this every time I grieve.

Grieving Husband

You just went to sleep, my darling,
And woke up in Heaven above,
Death did take you away from me,
But it can never end our love.

You will always be in my memory,
And one day, I'll see you again.
Lord, help my time here pass quickly,
I can hardly wait until then.

I must stay here a little longer,
And carry out God's perfect plan,
So I can live my life here in victory,
Trying to become a better man.

Then, one day when my time is over,
I, too, will walk those golden shores.
And I'll be ready to meet my Savior,
And I won't have to grieve any more.

Prayer

You don't have to visit my grave,
You know that I'm not there,
If you want to be close to me,
Come to Jesus, with a prayer.

Because when you talk to Him,
It's just like talking to me,
Because He and I are one now,
His love has set me free.

Don't grieve because I'm not there,
Why would you want me to be?
Life here is so wonderful,
You should feel real proud for me.

Turn My Spirit Loose

If you will turn my spirit loose,
Your grief will soon be released,
And you can start to live again,
Knowing I am at peace.

My time on earth has ended,
But I'll never cease to live.
I have such a wonderful life now,
So much better than earth could give.

I touched my Savior's hand today,
And I know that He is real,
So you must let my spirit go,
My future has been sealed.

You Fought the Fight

We loved you so,
You were the best.
You fought the fight,
Now you're at rest.
You brightened our day,
You made us smile.
You bravely walked,
Through every trial.

You Were So Strong

You never once complained, my love,
Even when you suffered so long.
No matter how fierce the pain,
You were always so very strong.

But Jesus knew just how you felt,
Because He, too, has suffered so.
He died so you could live again,
That's why I can let you go.

He knew that you loved Him so,
As He took you home to Him.
And I know that He knows best.
His ways I can't condemn.

So good-bye, my sweet darling,
I'll see you again before long.
I have a little more work here,
So ask God to make me strong.

Dear Wife

It's true and I must accept it,
You have entered a brand new life.
I know in my heart, you're at peace,
But oh, how I miss you, dear wife.

My thoughts just seem to confuse me,
Still I don't want them erased,
Because your beauty and kindness are still present,
As I try to picture your face.

Your hands were always busy.
You never idled your time.
But you were never too busy for me,
Oh, I'm so thankful you became mine.

So, good-bye, my sweet darling,
We'll be together again before too long.
So, I'll turn you over to God now.
I'm really trying to be strong.